D1320597

THE
CARDIJN STORY

THE
CARDIJN STORY

*A study of the life of Mgr. Joseph Cardijn
and the Young Christian Workers' Movement
which he founded*

BY

MICHAEL DE LA BEDOYERE

POSTULATE
ST. CATHERINE'S CONVENT

THE BRUCE PUBLISHING COMPANY
MILWAUKEE

THE BRUCE PUBLISHING COMPANY
400 NORTH BROADWAY, MILWAUKEE 1, WISCONSIN

This edition first published 1959

© MICHAEL DE LA BEDOYERE 1958

PRINTED IN GREAT BRITAIN BY BUTLER & TANNER LTD.,
FROME AND LONDON. NIHIL OBSTAT: CAROLUS DAVIS, S.T.L.,
CENSOR DEPUTATUS. IMPRIMATUR: E. MORROGH BERNARD,
VIC. GEN. WESTMONASTERII, DIE 7a FEBRUARII, 1958.

CONTENTS

ILLUSTRATIONS

AUTHOR'S FOREWORD

THE writing of these pages was suggested to me by the International President of the Young Christian Workers (Jeunesse Ouvrière Chrétienne), Pat Keegan, and the plan was approved by Mgr. Cardijn himself. Consequently, I have received all possible help in writing it from officials of the movement, here in Britain and abroad, and I have had the privilege of spending some time with Mgr. Cardijn himself who told me a great deal, especially about the early years of his life.

When the idea was suggested, I said: 'But surely there must be plenty of books already written about so famous a person as Mgr. Cardijn and about the Y.C.W.?' I was quite wrong. The Y.C.W., it seemed, had been much too busy getting on with its job to find time for biographies and studies. In fact, apart from a little (but very well done) forty-eight-page Canadian booklet, *Cardijn, Père de la J.O.C. Mondiale*, published anonymously in 1947, and some valuable typewritten notes for a Diploma in Social Science by Mlle L. Gemis, who was a full-time worker in the movement, nothing whatsoever existed. This extraordinary lack of self-contemplation, typical of the activist Y.C.W., made the idea of trying my hand all the more attractive, but it has not made the job easier. Anything like a full biography and study would in the circumstances have demanded a great deal of time, travel and consultation. As the editor of a weekly paper, the *Catholic Herald*, I have not been able to find the time necessary for any such ambitious project. This short book, in fact, is more like a free-lance effort in an inevitably difficult field. What I have tried to do is to convey to the ordinary reader what seems to me to be the personality and spirit of one of the most remarkable priests of our times and the way in which his movement has translated into fact and action the unique inspiration of its founder. I have also sought to set the story against the background of the times, in their ecclesiastical and social relevance, and to show how very much of the Church's contemporary spiritual leadership, concentrated as it is on the formation of an effective lay apostolate, is due to Mgr. Cardijn's initiative.

Even this limited objective could not have been accomplished—or at least accomplished in what I hope proves to be a lively and interesting way—without some hunting for the relevant biographical detail, especially during the early days when Mgr. Cardijn was feeling his way towards the realisation of the special vocation which was implanted within him. It also required a detailed study of the main phases of the Y.C.W. movement. Happily, if Mgr. Cardijn and his followers were uninterested in themselves, they were bound to express again and again their plans and ideas in written form and by the spoken word. Thanks to the help of the Y.C.W. International in Brussels, a considerable documentation was put at my disposal, much of it unpublished in other than typewritten form. The English reader, by the way, has at his disposal the valuable book *Challenge to Action*, in which Fr. Eugene Langdale has translated and edited some of Mgr. Cardijn's more important addresses. If my book does no more than draw wider attention to that inspiring publication, it will not have been written in vain.

Actually, only one full-dress serious book about the Y.C.W. seems to have been written. It is Marguerite Fièvez's *La Vie de Fernand Tonnet, Premier Jociste*. It has, of course, been invaluable, but one of the special secrets of the Y.C.W. is the relationship within it between the priest and the layman. Their work is complementary, yet the layman, who would be impotent without the priest, is the fully responsible, fully autonomous apostle. Mlle Fièvez therefore could properly write the life of the first Jocist with relatively little reference to Mgr. Cardijn. It was in fact the greatest compliment she could have paid to the movement's founder. The novel, _Fishers of Men_, by Maxence van der Meersch has been a best-seller on the Continent and must have made the Y.C.W. known to very many thousands who would not otherwise have heard of the movement; but though I have quoted some striking passages from it, the book does not greatly help the biographer and student.

I must thank Mlle Fièvez very particularly for all kinds of help which she has given, and thank also the other members of her staff in Brussels.

Let me end this note with one or two small points. The movement is naturally best known as the J.O.C., though the letters Y.C.W. become more familiar as it spreads in English-speaking countries. In this book I have used both according to the context. I have usually referred to the subject of the biography simply as Cardijn. This may be unusual in English books where living priests are usually given the 'Fr.' or 'Canon' or 'Mgr.' to which they are entitled. But I see Cardijn as somewhat removed from the accidents (and courtesies) of time and space—indeed as a force and inspiration who will long outlive his years on earth.

I have one great regret. In this book there are very few references to the J.O.C.F. as such, the women's section of the great movement. Mgr. Cardijn began with the girl apprentices of his parish in Brussels and he has never given them second place to the men. But constant reference to them would have involved much duplication. They must be assumed to be included on most occasions when the movement is mentioned. Perhaps Mlle Fièvez herself will one day write the book which will compensate for this discourtesy, unwilling as it has been.

Lastly, I would like to add that though this book tries to tell the story of a very great Catholic and of a Catholic movement, the apostolic and social inspiration of Mgr. Cardijn can be shared, to a large degree, by serious and enthusiastic Christians of all denominations. Mgr. Cardijn even said to me that his Movement could be adapted to Buddhists! The Y.C.W. net does not exclude non-Catholics and it has been adapted to other Communions. I hope, therefore, that Christians and social workers of all denominations, especially among young people, who may pick up this book will not feel that it has no message for them. The manuscript was read by Pat Keegan, who has recently resigned the International Presidency held for many fruitful years, Fr. Edward Mitchinson, National Chaplain in Britain, and Fr. Eugene Langdale. I have benefited greatly from their help and suggestions, and I thank them for the trouble they have taken.

Here is someone who talks to me of the masses, of saving the masses. Everyone else talks to me of the *élite*. *Pope Pius XI*

I am struck more every day by the extraordinary greatness of this enterprise. If Christian inspiration succeeds in penetrating economic and social forms, likely to live on, it will perhaps come to build up a firm and indefinitely perfectible civilisation. *Dr. Alexis Carrell in a letter to Cardijn*

This movement is the finest piece of youth work being done at the moment by the Christian Church. *Canon G. W. O. Addleshaw (C. of E.)*

There are so many things the world thinks impossible. The force of the good, properly organised, has yet to give the results that one may justifiably expect. We need more boldness to make the world happy. *Joseph Cardijn*

I

THE POOR BOY OF HAL
(1882–1906)

NEARLY seventy years ago a traveller visiting Belgium—
perhaps from Britain or America, perhaps from Italy or
France—might well have taken a train from Brussels to
spend an hour or two in the little town of Hal, some ten
miles south of the Belgian capital. Not that he would have
wished to visit Hal for its own sake, unless, maybe, he was
an industrialist interested to exploit the advantages of setting up some business in a growing town, so conveniently
situated on the line from Brussels to Paris. Aesthetically,
Hal was very much like dozens of small towns on the inter-
minable Belgian plain. Cobbled streets, crossing now and
then a dirty, sluggish river or canal, pushed their way between the solid banks of houses, variegated a little by the
different plaster colours—grey, brown, yellow, green, blue
—and by the large windows staring at the passer-by through
their contrastingly painted frames. Hal, lying on the southern edge of Flanders, might indeed have struck the visitor
walking from the station as an active and bustling town,
for a factory here or a mill there would remind him of the
rapid expansion of Belgian industry in those golden years
after the middle of the great century of progress and prosperity—years when the peasants left their fields and their
cottage trades to work in the growing towns where a labour
force, increasing itself three times, was enabling its employers to increase their production and profit no less than seven
times.

Our visitor, however, would be rapidly walking the few hundred yards from the dirty coal-smeared station, crossing the bridges, where a few sad trees seemed to be resigned to a twisted and stunted growth in the face of the competition of a world of brick and iron. Past the little shops he would hurry, following the curve of the streets until suddenly the narrow way opened on to a *grande place*, the heart of the old town where the object of his pilgrimage stood before him. To the left of him it rose, the great Gothic bell-tower, not unfittingly surmounted in this Flanders land by the baroque cupola. Tall, too, in the northern Gothic way, with long sloping roof, was the church, its ancient stone worn and fretted by the centuries to harmonise with the intricate patterns which the ancestors of the factory workers of modern Hal had fashioned in praise of the Blessed Virgin, who had so singularly blessed their town with the favours prayed for at the foot of her miraculous statue, now standing above the high altar.

Notre Dame de Hal is not a three-star monument of Belgium, but it is a worthy edifice to enshrine the famous statue, given to Hal by the Countess of Holland and Zeeland in the thirteenth century. Hal soon became a centre of pilgrimage, and great princes—the Emperor himself, Edward III of England (in honour of his wife Philippa of Hainault), the Duke of Brabant, the daughter of Philip the Bold of Burgundy, and many others—helped the privileged people of Hal to build the church that stands today dominating the little town.

On his way to or from the famous church, our visitor might well, in the late eighties of the last century, have brushed past a little fair-haired boy of eight or nine, as likely as not busily shovelling coal as he helped his father to take the load from the railway truck to the homes which placed their orders with Henri Cardijn, Coal Merchant. Would he have noticed the boy, face and hands blackened by a job which only a child could really enjoy—that is, unless, as with this boy, the job had to be done time and time again, even in the face of the bitter winds which sweep unchecked across the endless flats from the north-east? Had he done so, he might have been struck by the lively eyes, the intelligent expression, pugnacious and mischievous, yet surely self-possessed, keenly observant, strong, good. At any rate, that little boy was destined—to put it at its lowest—to rescue the obscure, but in those parts common, name of Cardijn from the oblivion which it had suffered for generation after generation. Because of him, people have since sought to trace back the clan and to discover its origins in the Spanish Cardino—a possible explanation in view of the many years of Spanish rule in those parts. Maybe some such explanation is needed. How otherwise account for the imagination, vision and mystique which this son of an illiterate Flemish peasant— 'the last of men', as the elegant Parisian Fénelon was to describe the Flemings of his flock—would display in his life's work?

The phenomenon has also found explanation in a reputed Italian origin of the boy's mother. Here, alas, hard facts contradict the desirable explanation, for his mother, an equally Flemish Van Daele from Denderwindeke, near Alost, could only bring to her son such Italian sparkle as she could derive from the vineyards near Livorno which her father looked after as steward and where she was born. The Van Daeles were clearly a cut above the Cardijns, in the social sense, and experienced something of the pioneer spirit of the nineteenth century. This emigration to Italy on the part of the little boy's maternal grandfather was matched by his uncle who sailed across the world to Australia as a telegraphist. It was these widening horizons which were in tune with the sharper eyes, the mobile little face, the small thin wiry body of the boy who, as he was to confess much later, liked nothing better in those days than to rush with his companions along the streets, loudly ring a door-bell and then fly off, content to have awakened from an after-dinner nap some dull Flemish burgher. Much awakening of the somnolent and self-contented was to be done by that boy in the years to come. And many an angry face would emerge from its comfort, spiritual and temporal, to tell him to mind his own business.

Joseph was the boy's name, given him in baptism on 16 November 1882 at the font in the church of Saint-Servais, a few days after his birth on 13 November in Schaerbeek, then almost a suburb of Brussels, today a constituent part of the capital. The *curé* of Saint-Servais would hardly have looked twice at the infant brought to the church by its father, a coachman to a large house in the chaussée de Haecht, awkwardly dressed in his Sunday best. The mother, a servant, neighbour to the Cardijns in Hal, had not recovered from the effects of the child's birth. There was nothing for it then but to take baby Joseph to the Van Daele home in Hal to be cared for by his mother's relations.

A year or two later, after the birth of another child, Henri and Louise Cardijn were in a position to exchange their lowly domestic position in Schaerbeek and return to Hal to work on their own in the little coal business, negotiated, presumably, in the capital. There in a little house, next door to the Van Daele home, the family came together again: father, mother, Jeanne the eldest, Marie who died young, Joseph, and after him Victor and Charles.

And this is where we return to the dominance of the famous church which rises high above the little town, the church with its miraculous statue of Our Lady. For the Cardijns and the Van Daeles were God-fearing folk, descended from generations of solid Flemish Catholics. That the father could neither read nor write his native Flemish

Henry Cardijn, earlier a coachman and then a coal merchant of Hal, in Southern Flanders, the father of Joseph.

Louise Cardijn was born a Van Daele. It was next door to her family that the Cardijn coal business was set up soon after the birth of Joseph.

Joseph Cardijn is in the bottom right-hand corner of this school group.

At the seminary. Joseph is in the middle of the picture.

Wigan in the late 1930s. In the centre are Pat Keegan, Fr. Rimmer and Fr. Joseph Cardijn.

tongue, that the mother, by modern standards, had received but a smattering of education—these defects made but little difference, for the children were brought up from the first in the living school of the *lived* Christian tradition.

Of an evening, the children, having been got ready to go to bed, would patter into the living room and, snugly wrapped around, would squat by the great stove, while their mother taught them the story of the Bible as only a mother can. 'Even before I went to school I knew the whole of sacred history, and I knew it because my mother taught me. Just as my flesh comes from her, so does my mind. You are made by your mother.'[1] Such was Joseph Cardijn's later tribute to her. These lessons, vivid as they must have been, did not mean that there were no lighter moments with the traditional fairy-tales, for Louise Cardijn's temperament was as broad as her son's was later to prove. He himself would remember that his mother did not order. She just presented the case, the better against the bad, the best against the better. That little sum of money could be spent, could be saved, or it could be given to that poor man over there. The child had every choice—yet no choice, if he was to be worthy of his mother. 'The poorest mother can do it', as he was much later to teach.[2]

On the eve of Sundays and the feasts, the children would be taught in no less fascinating a way the meaning and prayers of the next day's liturgy, for how can one worship intelligently without understanding? Like all Christian children, these, too, would look forward to the preparations for Christmas with the little home crib and the coloured candles, humbly echoing the great crib and the lights of the church. But Christmas, Candlemas, Easter lived for them in their scriptural and liturgical setting, not as isolated sentimentalities. Against such a family background, the great

---

[1] *La Personne, La Famille, L'Education* (1950), pp. 25, 26.
[2] Ibid., p. 35.

B

church, only a short run away, with its high altar so often
ablaze with the light of the serried candles to honour the
little oak statue, blackened by the centuries, vested in
wondrous dresses of satin and gold, seized the imaginations
of such well-instructed deeply Catholic children. Every so
often, pilgrims flocked into Hal for the great pilgrimages
and the crowds made the spiritual tour of the town, pausing
by each of the forty-five little shrines—or, on lesser occasions,
walked in procession within the streets, or simply honoured
their patron within the walls of the church whose high-
vaulted interior with its statues, chapels, ambulatory, endless nooks and corners must have been a fairy-like home
from home for any imaginative boy.

It was a wonderful upbringing, but not, except for the
imaginative gifts of the mother and the stiff, sturdy faith of
the father, a privileged one. Hal was a Catholic town and
its many children shared such spiritual advantages. It was
Joseph Cardijn who was going to profit so outstandingly
from its setting.

For the moment it was school and manual work. His
parents had set their hearts on his having the chances
which they themselves had missed. At about six, he went
to a little convent school. At eleven he made his First
Communion, and afterwards he was transferred to a private
school which today is run by the Christian Brothers. But
one does not easily catch up with the slow start which is all
that uneducated parents can manage. Joseph started late
and progressed slowly, but we may guess that the shrewd
intuition which was native to him enabled him to profit
from the combination natural to him and others in those
times of sitting on a school bench and helping his parents to
make both ends meet in the intervals. Not only would he
have been seen with the little coal business, but doing the
early morning rounds with milk and vegetables produced
at the neighbouring Van Daele home which boasted a

garden and a small dairy. He must have slept well at nights.

Poverty in the sense of semi-destitution such as was far from unknown in Hal with the bad times that had succeeded the golden years, was not the fate of the Cardijns and Van Daeles, and we may be thankful for it, for that kind of poverty is not a good school for the leaders of the next generations. They could live, as men and women should live, with sufficient but certainly not too much, and they had to work desperately hard. The family was lucky, too, in that their country had started, slowly enough however, along the road of elementary social reform. But only by a short head had Joseph Cardijn missed being of the company of those children described by Fr. Vermeesch, recalling his days as a young seminarian:

> We can still see them—how could we forget them even after twenty-five years—those little unhealthy boys, on a beautiful summer evening, passing us at about six o'clock, on the out-skirts of an industrial town. We were returning home refreshed by a delightful walk along the river Meuse. They, pale and thin, carrying their little billy-cans in their left hand, were hurrying towards a factory. They were about 11 years old. 'Where are you going to?' we asked them. 'To the glass factory.' 'Till when?' 'Till six tomorrow morning.' Harsh indeed are the needs of industrial competition.

But if children had just come to be protected by the State from such cruel demands of wealth-making industrialism, Joseph Cardijn, like the mass of the children of Hal, could not expect to escape from the need at the age of twelve to help support his parents from the small wages to be earned in a factory at Hal or even, perhaps, by joining the band of commuters who were already daily crowding at the station to their work in Brussels itself.

We may be sure that he faced the prospect with courage and would not have sought to shirk responsibilities clearly falling on him. But already strange ideas were passing through the head of the boy who, to his father's astonishment, actually read books for the pleasure and profit of just reading.

An abyss was opening up between the two generations, between an excellent, but illiterate peasant father whose kind could be traced back in Flanders and all over Europe through the decades and the centuries, essentially unchanged, and the boy, stepping forward towards a new world of universal education, of seemingly boundless achievement, of the destruction of time and space and, with them, the ancient categories which divided men according to status and place. The Van Daeles had already been slightly affected. Not so the Cardijns. Yet the Cardijns, no less than the Van Daeles, played their part in inspiring the boy, even at so young an age, to feel that the abyss between two worlds had to be bridged if disaster to men was to be avoided. They did so because both had contributed to that deep Catholic formation which, under the protection of the Virgin of Hal, had given immediate direction to the boy's mind and feelings. In church, perhaps, or elsewhere in grown-up conversation, he had already heard tell about a revolutionary letter sent to the whole world by the Pope of Rome, Leo XIII. It was about the new state of things in the world and it said that it was all wrong for the masses of young and old who went daily to work in factories and workshops, whether in Hal or Brussels, to find themselves in a different moral world from the world of their families, their parishes, their Christian schools. It said that every man possessed a moral dignity which mattered as much in the textile, shoe-making, chemical, artificial silk factories as in their homes. This was common sense; it was natural. Yet already Joseph was noticing with shock and dismay how the facts of life pointed the opposite way and heard his parents talking about it. Those who had been his friends but a year or two back were already starting their life's work in such factories. And how they had changed! They had been coarsened. They used filthy language. They told stories of the degrading practices taken for granted within the world of the workers. Religion, church, the pieties of the home, these were quickly being thrown aside now that they had been initiated into the modern worker's estate within the daily, brutalising grind of repetitive work. It was the same for the girls, and the realisation was all the harsher to a boy who so worshipped his mother. Children and parents, as he later recounted, had grown so far apart as barely to know one another.

The abyss which separated a Christian home from the outside world was not in itself a new phenomenon. For years even quite little children had been sent from home to work long hours to help their parents' dwindling income in an age when home industry was dying out; children who would return so worn and dispirited as to refuse to be comforted on their mothers' laps. And since the 1880s and 1890s in Flanders up till the present time the abyss has often remained. It was accepted as inevitable before; by many a good Christian it is accepted today as inevitable. Yet, mysteriously, to this not so well-educated boy of Hal the paradox was already presenting itself as a personal challenge, through his vivid sense of the change in those who had been his friends. Why this should have been so is part of the mystery of human vocation, sensibility, drive, character, which causes one to be chosen from among so many who, often apparently better equipped in mind and talent, are content to allow life to lead them instead of feeling the call to lead it.

Joseph Cardijn, awakened so early to a deeply disturbing fact which others took for granted, naturally reacted to it in the simplest Catholic way. The solution could only come from the Church and he must be of the Church, of the men called and dedicated to live and spread the Gospel of Christ beyond the safe bounds of home and parish, bounds created to preserve the *bien-pensants* from the abyss that divides not only the past from the future, not only the protected from the unprotected, but even the Sunday and family side of a Christian man and woman's life from the contradictory weekday life.

Naturally, the boy could not then see things in these adult terms, but the astonishing continuity and unchanged purpose of his life's work must force the observer to the conclusion that somehow that child's vision of his priestly vocation, stimulated by an as yet uncomprehended experience, contained within it the seed of all that was to come.

Conflict in his mind between the duty to go to work, as the eldest boy called to be the breadwinner of tomorrow, and the unexpected stirrings within him, must have been deep and costly, for it seems that he was unable to whisper a word of it even to his mother. The days passed and all was prepared for him to begin work as an apprentice. He would start next morning.

'The night before I was to leave for the factory', he wrote twenty-seven years later, 'I went upstairs with my brothers and sisters. When all were asleep, I came down barefooted to the kitchen where my father and mother were still chatting, although it was already late.'

He tip-toed over to them and said to his father, 'Papa, I must ask you something. Can I carry on with my studies?'

'But you're the eldest, you know it well enough,' his astonished father retorted. 'You're the eldest and your mother and I are counting on you to help us bring up your brothers and sisters.'

Then he had to break his real news.

'I feel that God is calling me, I want to become a priest.'

Henri Cardijn was shocked. He was getting on and after

a hard life he had a right to expect his eldest son to learn to take over his responsibilities. There was silence. Then he looked at his wife and perhaps from her drew the courage to say: 'Well, we've certainly worked hard enough already, but we will go on working, poor as we are, if we are to have this blessing.'

So it was then and there decided that Joseph should continue in his school until the time came for him to go to Malines.

It was at the age of fourteen, in 1896, that he entered the Petit-Seminaire of Malines. The words Petit-Seminaire should not, however, be misunderstood. Joseph was indeed studying with a view to beginning in about three years' time ecclesiastical training, but in this he was among the minority, for the school was open to all boys, and it would be seven years before he would be wearing clerical dress. At Malines he was for the present a boy among boys, and he went home to Hal for his holidays, one week at Christmas, two at Easter, and six during the summer. Life had not greatly altered, except that that first shock and challenge caused by the change in friends who had become young workers was soon deepened. The student who came back to Hal for his holidays was no longer a troubled little boy distressed by the change that had come over his old friends and determined to do all he could to solve the puzzle; he was now in the eyes of his friends the enemy. He had gone over to the other side, to the Church and the priests and the fairy-tales.

I could see then how my old playmates—better chaps than I, often enough—had given up even going to church after a few months at work. Just because I was studying to be a priest, they looked upon me as an enemy. The abyss between us had been dug. How could this change be explained, I kept on asking myself. It isn't that there is anything intrinsically evil in the working class itself. Anyway, it's a better class than many others. In this way, I realised that these young people had virtually no choice but to founder within the environment of their work. This was my first revelation about the real facts of the young workers' lives. From that moment onwards I was haunted, haunted for life, by the call: to save the working class. I could see that endless procession of young people, thirteen or fourteen years old, forced to leave school in order to work in corrupt conditions. After a few months of this they were unrecognisable. They had been given an entirely false idea of work, of girls, of dates, of love, of marriage. The truth was that entirely new problems were raised by these young people of thirteen and fourteen, and there was no one to help them to find the right answer.[1]

It is worth dwelling for a moment on the words 'It isn't that there is anything intrinsically evil in the working class itself. Anyway, it's a better class than many others.' The schoolboy had sure-footedly taken the right—and the rare —step forward. Assimilated to the inevitably bourgeois character of a Catholic and clerical boarding school, he had instinctively avoided the temptation of seeing the workers as a class apart to be pitied and, if possible, helped by their betters. That temptation must have been especially strong in those days, seeing how easily people succumb to it even today, for then the mass of the *bien-pensants* were still directly affected by the Calvinist or Puritan idea that success in business and life was the reward for the godly virtues of hard work, saving, self-discipline, whereas poverty was the fruit of heedlessness, spending, self-indulgence. Instinctively, the boy saw that there was nothing wrong with the workers but what they suffered from their so-called betters. The workers were victims of a bad system; their employers often its active agents. Only afford them the chance of being men and women, of being responsible persons, of being Christians, and there would be no workers'

[1] *La J.O.C. École de Vie* (1947), pp. 10, 11.

problem, no proletariat. Joseph Cardijn, a lifetime ahead of most of those with whom he worked and played at Malines, so many of whom shared with him the priestly calling, has laboured a lifetime to teach that essential truth in the face of constant opposition.

Looking back, at the age of sixty-seven, Joseph Cardijn, risen then from Monsieur l'Abbé to Monsieur le Chanoine and from Monsieur le Chanoine to Monseigneur, could say of those days:

> I am sixty-seven today. They tell me I am still young. True enough, I am a young man of sixty-seven—younger than I was at twenty or thirty or even forty. At thirteen years of age, I grasped the real problem—forty-four years ago. I am the son of a poor working man who could neither read nor write—the son of a mother who, from her earliest years, was, first, a domestic servant, then a concierge at Schaerbeek, rue d'Haecht, then a working woman by the day in houses. It was my destiny also to become a working man, but my mother and father made the sacrifices which enabled me to go on with my studies. I went to the seminary; but when I left it for my holidays I saw again my old friends. At school, they were more pious and cleverer than I, who was not first in my class. They had entered the factory and were already corrupted, lost. They no longer went to church. I vowed that this would not go on. That's how the J.O.C. started.[1]

These years of adolescent schooling do not seem to have left any notable memories, for Joseph Cardijn was not a scholar. He was a boy of action and displayed plenty of initiative outside rather than inside the schoolroom. But his initiative and his interests found more scope in the freedom of holiday-time than in the then severe discipline of a clerical college. As he grew older, he began to do things, to fight for causes which appealed to him, instinctively to find means of training himself for the cause to which he

[1] *Ibid.*

would devote his life. In Hal, for example, he would give himself over to active help for the good causes promoted in the town. He enjoyed acting and liked to produce plays which would bring in the needed francs and sous. He joined the union of students, interesting it already in the cause of the workers, and took his place on the public platform, thus training himself as a speaker and defending what he believed to be right. From the start he devoted himself to the Flemish cause. Flemish language, literature and consciousness had declined in the eighteenth century and might well, it seemed, have been finally killed with the creation of French-speaking modern Belgium in 1830. But in reaction to the imposition of French by the government, the Flemish movement quickly grew to establish the two 'nations' who found a common loyalty only in service to Belgium and its monarch. Flanders was, and has remained, steadfastly Catholic; Walloon or French-speaking Belgium was deeply affected by the anti-clericalism and secularism of France. Doubly, then, as a Fleming and as a devoted Catholic, Joseph Cardijn worked for the Flemish cause and was to do so for many years. The importance of this lies, perhaps, not so much in the nature of the cause itself, as in the indication it gives of the activist and political bent of his mind and character. Political in this context is not to be interpreted as party-political, but as a natural interest in the *polis*, the aims and values of the temporal organisation of which he was a member. This early taste and training was to play a valuable part in his life's work, in that he was always to see very clearly two things: the Christian importance of what was happening to people in their political and social relationships, in their lives, in their work; and the proper distinction between the spiritual sphere of the Church and the temporal sphere of the civic authorities and civic and social organisations which derived from social interests.

Joseph Cardijn's purpose to become a priest was at no time shaken during these years, and he passed from scholastic studies to the philosophical and theological studies in the Malines seminary which led directly to his ordination.

It was in the year when he first wore the soutane or clerical dress—in 1903—that he received a telegram to tell him that his father was seriously ill. He has told how he set off at once for his home to find his father worn out and near death. His father raised his wrinkled old hand and gave his son kneeling by the bedside his blessing. 'It is about forty-four years since I said by the bedside of my father who killed himself that I might become a priest: "Father, you killed yourself for me; I shall kill myself to save the working class of the world." '

His early boyhood impressions of the change that working-class life made on his little friends; the scandal he took at finding himself in the ranks of 'the enemy of the workers'; the sacrifices his father had made for him: for Joseph Cardijn they all added up to one thing—an absolute resolution to find the ways and means of ensuring for the workers of his country and of the world (for Joseph Cardijn's faith had no limits) lives as human and as full, and therefore lives as Christian, as those taken for granted by their so-called betters.

But his deepest and fullest dedication was made on 22 September 1906, when the recently appointed Archbishop of Malines, Mgr. Mercier, ordained Joseph Cardijn priest.

Looking from outside at the character of the young man of twenty-four, stamped now and for ever with the powers and mission of the priesthood, one may feel a certain surprise that his vocation had taken this turn. His more obvious characteristics, of an intensively activist nature linked with an ardent concern over the conditions of the workers, over social and political questions; his extroverted nature that loved doing, seizing concrete situations, expressing itself in talking, teaching, helping; even that flame within him that fed a single-minded zeal for a visibly better world, and this without delay—all these suggested the future lay leader, the fighter in the market-place, the social reformer and political figure destined visibly to wield power. No doubt, it might have been. But the religious vocation had to come to him in early boyhood, and much of the fascination and uniqueness of his life have derived from the spiritual intensity of that priestly vocation applied uncompromisingly, yet in a completely priestly way, to the temporal, social causes which from the first he had held so dear. The rare combination, which, so easily misunderstood, would cause much opposition and even scandal, was to ensure the almost unique characteristic of his movement, one in which the primacy of the spiritual and the vital role of the priest were to remain consistent with the complete responsibility and autonomy of the worker-leaders; like acting on like, as it was to be expressed.

In order to understand this better, we may leave for the moment the newly-ordained Abbé Cardijn and picture for ourselves the social and economic conditions within which the young priest was for a long time to plan and to give battle before the beginnings of success came his way.

2

THE YOUNG PRIEST AND HIS WORLD
(1906–1912)

SPEAKING in 1939 during a Study Conference at Godinne, Joseph Cardijn, having talked about apostasies in the history of Christianity, went on:

> There is another kind of apostasy. In States with free governments—in Belgium, France, England, the United States, in most countries, in fact—there is to be found an unconscious, anonymous apostasy that began with liberalism. First, earthly life and its organisation were separated off from the idea of God, from God's authority and from religion. Then the view was taken that the State, that public and private institutions should be neutral and unconcerned about God, religion and eternal truths. These basic and eternal realities were to be left to individual consciences without bothering about how they related to actual present life, individual, family, professional, national and international. Under the influence of liberalism, materialism, sensuality, the attraction of pleasure and the distractions of different kinds of enjoyment, the people in their masses have been gradually drawn along so that we have reached the stage when it may be said that the apostasy of the masses threatens to become universal.[1]

This divorce between the temporal and the spiritual—a long and slow process, which began before the Reformation with the first great economic revolution, caused by the sudden widening of Christian horizons with the discovery of the new worlds to the East and to the West, and established itself in the nineteenth century with the great Industrial Revolution—was the great heresy of the West. The medieval Catholic Church had taught that money-making for its own sake, covetousness, avarice, were deadly sins in exactly the same way as we today regard adultery as a sin about which there can be no argument, and it did so because it regarded economics as necessarily and directly subject to the spiritual end of man.

> The medieval theorist condemned as a sin precisely that effort to achieve the continuous and unlimited increase in material wealth which modern societies applaud as a quality, and the vices for which he reserved his most merciless denunciations were the more refined and subtle of the economic virtues. 'He who has enough to satisfy his wants,' wrote a Schoolman of the fourteenth century, 'and nevertheless ceaselessly labours to acquire riches, either in order to obtain a higher social position, or that subsequently he may have enough to live without labour, or that his sons may become men of wealth and importance—all such are incited by a damnable avarice, sensuality and pride.' [1]

The echo of that medieval teaching once again reached the ears of the world generally—and even of the great majority of Catholics in the world—only when Joseph Cardijn was nine years old and Pope Leo XIII issued his encyclical *Rerum Novarum*, applying the self-same principle that every aspect of economic life—now so different from the medieval social pattern—remained subject to God and the spiritual end of every man.

In the hundred years before Cardijn was born the Industrial Revolution had challenged the consciences of men through bringing into being what we call the working classes—what Marx called the proletariat. Cardijn himself has described the process in simple and popular terms.

[1] R. H. Tawney: *Religion and the Rise of Capitalism*, p. 35.

The working class, as it exists today, has only existed for 150 years [he said in 1948]. Its life has been short. It is very young. It began when the steam engine was invented. That invention brought about the industrial and the economic revolution—a revolution in the method of work and production. So important is this revolution that, from the social, religious and human point of view, its consequences are such as still to be unpredictable in their scope and their total reaction. The invention of the steam-engine brought into the world the so-called mechanical work. The steam-engine was converted into a gas-engine. Then petrol, then heavy oil, then electricity—and tomorrow atomic power—drove engines displacing the labour of thousands and even millions of men. Therefore it is the invention of the steam-engine which has created the world's working class as it exists today. In doing so, it created the problem of the workers. In creating the problem of the workers, it gave birth to the movement of the workers. Do not let people deceive you by saying that all this is communism. Communism has nothing to do with it. The communists came much later. Don't let them say 'He talks like a communist.' It is not true: a working class, a workers' problem, a movement of the workers, all these exist independently of communism and socialism.

Before the machine was invented everyone walked. There were no trains, autocars and bicycles. When I was a boy there were no bicycles. At the end of the last century, they were invented. What excitement when we first saw one. Today everybody has one. Then everyone had to walk from his home to his job—sometimes to walk thirty miles—hours of walking before working!

And the speaker, applying all these facts to the problems of today, showed how the little workshop grew into the business; how capital was a necessary element in the business; how the use of the modern machine is responsible for the fact that an ever-greater number of human beings in the world are and will remain wage-earners.

That is how it all came about. Little by little, from 1769 to

1848, the working class was born in the different countries of Europe. From England to Belgium, France, Holland, Germany and all the countries of the world. These workers had no voice. They stood at the factory gates. 'Is there work?'—'Yes, over there.'—'How much?'—'So much an hour.'—'Until when?'—'Till such an hour.'—'Not good enough?'—'Well, if you don't like it, clear out.' [1]

Thus, the two elements came together. The invention of the machine, in itself a good thing since it promised a much higher level of living for men, went hand in hand with a moral outlook which had come completely to deny that there was any relationship between the economic order and the spiritual nature of every human being. The indefinitely increased productive power of man went hand in hand with the conscious or unconscious apostasy that denied the relevance of God and the spiritual order to the temporal order of politics and economics.

Economic liberalism led to the suppression of all professional organisations on behalf of the famous law of economic liberty, of science, progress and absolute freedom. Not only suppression, but formal interdiction. The workers were forbidden to join together, to group themselves, to combine for wages and hours of work. Those who tried to do so were clapped into prison and condemned. When they dared to strike, soldiers intervened, fired on them and killed some of them. And economic liberalism became political liberalism. The State became the policeman guarding order, making sure that liberty was observed, watching to see that the workers did not combine or assemble or work one another up. And economic and political liberalism likewise became religious liberalism. They said: this has nothing to do with the Church. The Church's business is within the churches and the sacristies. Its business has nothing to do with wages and working conditions. If you say so, you're a clerical. The Church and religion are out of all this. And Catholics, Catholic employers,

[1] *L'Heure de la Classe Ouvrière* (1948), Stenograph edition, pp. 3–8.

The founder of the J.O.C. and his English right-hand man, Pat Keegan.

Pope Pius XII welcomes Mgr. Cardijn with whom is an English Y.C.W. girl, Margaret Ridden.

Cardijn the priest, in Rome in 1957.

learned Catholics let themselves be influenced by the liberalism of the times. Deceived by the economic, political, philosophical and religious liberalism they allowed the wool to be
pulled over their eyes and they abandoned the working class.

Thus it came about that, from 1848 onwards, led by socialist and communist leaders, the workers and the workers'
movement were used as a tool against the Church. Deceived
in its misery and in the way it was exploited, the working
class was, little by little, turned away from the Church, and
then detached from it. Because economic liberalism weighed
so heavily on the working class, Leo XIII called its condition
'a new slavery'.[1]

By the first decade of the twentieth century when Joseph
Cardijn was ordained and embarking on his life's vocation,
certain Christians, both Catholic and Protestant, had come
to realise far better the nature of the moral, social and
political challenge of the Industrial Revolution to Christianity. But it had inevitably been a very slow growth.
After all, Christianity in Europe had been powerfully
shaken by the growth of secularist humanism, of what perhaps is best described as 'progressivism', in every aspect of
life—in philosophy and science, in culture, in politics and
now in economics, technique and industry. To all that the
French Revolution had meant in an anti-clerical break-up
of the old order was now added this tremendous sweep of
scientific, industrial and political emancipation from the
feudal *ancien régime*, so closely associated with Christian
leadership and patronage.

Instinctive Christian reactions were, at first, extra-
ordinarily piecemeal and muddled. While a Lammenais in
France, as early as 1830, anticipated by a century much of
the Christian Democratic ideal of today, leaving, after his
condemnation for exaggerated views, only traces of his constructive influence, Christians, as individuals, accepted

[1] Op. cit., pp. 9, 10.

C

uncritically the liberal outlook in economics and business. And among the minority which began to have a 'conscience' about the fate of the growing working class, the tendency, both among clergy and laity, was a feudal one. The workers had to be protected against themselves; they had to be amused and distracted; they had to be relieved by good works; they had to be educated; above all, they had to be kept faithful and, if possible, pious. They were the responsibility of 'the ruling class', of their 'betters'. The idea that there was a Christian answer to the social and economic problem in terms of a Christian political and social alternative to the ideology of the day was still quite foreign, even to those most concerned with the state of the world. It was in fact the growth of socialism of a positive anti-clerical nature which caused a minority of Catholics to look at the Church for an alternative, for positive Christian social ideology rooted in an increasing loyalty to the position and leadership of the Popes, while the majority looked to the Church more and more as a protection against the increasing threat of social revolution.

Nor were the Christians of those times altogether to be blamed for the slowness of their reactions. The whole situation presented a new and difficult problem. How was the traditional distinction between Church and State, between the spiritual and temporal order, to be applied in this totally new situation? What was the precise status of the clergy in regard to the social, as distinct from the religious, problem of the masses? What was the status of the lay Catholic reformer, of the working-class leader, in relation to the Church's doctrinal and moral authority? What was the status of the Catholic politician, the Catholic party, offering a political solution intended to mobilise secular forces, in relation to the priest and to the exclusivist doctrine of Catholicism generally? Only by slow growth and experience could these problems be worked out and a practical Christian democratic and social alternative to the parties of the Right and of the Left be shaped.

It was just about the time when Joseph Cardijn was born —in the 1880s—that sufficient experience and initiative were obtained to express themselves in genuine Catholic workers' movements based on a real Christian synthesis compounded of the good in liberalism and a much deeper understanding of man than collectivist theories could offer. But it was a slow, painful, much criticised growth in the face of a bourgeois world—and the clerical world was, in these matters, virtually a bourgeois world also—for which any workers' autonomy, let alone trade-union organisation in itself, was dangerous and to be resisted. Only slowly could there be, especially where the Church was officially concerned, development from a semi-religious, patronising and anti-socialist conception of Christian workers' unity to the realisation of an independent and militant programme in defence of the workers' rights and for the attainment of a workers' status consonant with human dignity and responsibility and the legitimate aspirations of one of the two great partners in growing industrial enterprise. One learns with some surprise, for example, that by 1913, when Joseph Cardijn, as we shall see, was pioneering a new approach to working youth, there were only 102,000 members in the Christian Trade Unions in Belgium and only 126,000 in the Socialist. The idea of a mass movement, of the realisation of worker solidarity and (for the Christian) of a specialised and autonomous workers' vocation within the social pattern was still well ahead.

It was therefore within a bourgeois and a still predominantly liberal world, clerical and lay, a world run by the 'betters' with no more than a slightly sharpened sensitivity about the rights and status of the tiresome masses, that Joseph Cardijn was ordained and given priestly authority and influence in carrying out his life's vocation to save the Christian workers for Christianity by saving them as men, individually and within their workers' status, dignity and responsibility.

The young priest's interests were sufficiently clearly defined—and no wonder—to cause Archbishop Mercier to send him for a year's study to his own Faculty of Philosophy at Louvain and the School of Political and Social Sciences which depended on it. One may guess that the theoretical courses taught by professors brought up in a world that was passing away did not make a very great impression on the young priest who, at best, was never a scholar and a theorist, but an experimentalist. It may be that he himself, never hesitant in expressing his own views, made a greater impression on them—and this by no means always a favourable one. 'We were good friends, however,' he said, recalling those days. But it was not to any faculty of sociology that Abbé Cardijn would graduate; it was to the humbler status of schoolmaster in the Petit-Seminaire of Basse-Wavre that he was appointed after a year at Louvain. This Petit-Seminaire was the Walloon counterpart to the Malines Petit-Seminaire where he himself had been schooled. Like Malines it must be regarded as an ordinary secondary school with its quota of students hoping to be trained for the priesthood.

Whether accidentally or by design, Louvain and Basse-Wavre afforded him exactly the experience and training that he required, the experience and training which were, in fact, to condition much of his future work. The long holidays gave him the opportunity of studying abroad the real conditions of the workers and what was actually being done for them, while the teaching at Basse-Wavre brought him into an infinitely valuable formative contact with youth, the lessons of which he has never forgotten and which indeed have been applied throughout his life to the Young Christian Workers.

His first journey abroad was made to Germany and it took place while he was in Louvain. It was natural that he should go to Germany, a country at that time closely linked with Belgium and especially with Flanders. The Ruhr and Rhineland comprise, together with southern Holland and northern Belgium, the north bastion of a traditionally Catholic belt of territory that runs down to Austria and Northern Italy. And Germany had, in many ways, as compared with France, pioneered Catholic social thinking in the new age and organisations designed to meet the new needs. Michael Fogarty has excellently summarised the work of Bishop Ketteler whose thinking paved the way for Leo XIII's *Rerum Novarum*.

Bishop Ketteler is the outstanding figure of the whole German Catholic social movement. He began his career as an army officer and civil servant, but resigned from the civil service as a protest against the incidents of 1837 and entered the Church when the Archbishop of Cologne was imprisoned for defying the State's ruling about Church matters. After serving as curate and parish priest he was elected to the German National Assembly at Frankfurt in 1848, and made his mark there. At the end of the same year he preached in the cathedral of Mainz a series of sermons which have been described as 'a preliminary sketch of the whole doctrine of the Catholic social movement'. Then and thereafter, he marked off Christian social doctrine from liberalism by insisting on the social responsibilities of property, on the dangers of an 'atomised' society, and on the evil effects of unlimited competition, particularly in reducing labour to the status of a commodity. Against the rising Socialist movement he insisted on the need for a wide distribution of property and the dangers of exaggerated State control. Against both he claimed that the social question is primarily moral and religious. . . . In general, he supported strongly the idea of workers forming their own associations for self-help, and demanded a wide range of social reforms to be realised either in this way or through the State: higher wages, profit-sharing, reasonable working hours, weekly rest days, factory inspection, and special regulation of women's and children's work.[1]

More directly relevant to Cardijn, doubtless, was the work of Fr. Adolf Kolping who foreshadowed a 'Christian Workers' Movement' half a century or more before Cardijn. But the Kolping Associations, while so far ahead of their time, were not a workers' movement in the modern sense, either in their scope or in their object. They were for young craftsmen rather than for the masses and the work was educational rather than social. But Kolping was outstanding in seeing from the first the importance of the workers' formation for a man in his working secular life as well as in his spiritual. Later in the century, factory workers were admitted, though the rules were made tighter and more restrictive, and only in the present century did the government of the Associations partially pass out of clerical hands.

In actual fact, Joseph Cardijn does not seem to have referred in his speeches and writings to the Kolping precedent, so we may hazard the view that, as with the Scout movement a little later, his instinct told him that this was not what he was seeking. From the very start, his focus was that working class as such into which, as he had seen as a child, good men and women were absorbed to be spiritually —and often bodily—prostituted. The working class must save the working class. Like must save like. Everything was to be 'with them, by them, for them'.

Typically, he devoted much of his time in Cologne, Düsseldorf, Essen, Münster and the Ruhr to a close study of the *facts* of different industries, to mining, to the textile industries, to toy-making; and this fact-finding—to be the essential preliminary to all judgment and action in his life —led him to read all he could lay his hands on, so as to

---

[1] *Christian Democracy and Western Europe*, pp. 164–5.

form a living picture not so much of the industrial processes as of the fate of the men, women and children whose lives depended on their work within them.

In articles in the *Revue Sociale Catholique* of Louvain in 1907, he gathered together his findings. Thus he writes:

> Those who weave at home instead of at a factory are submitted to an excessively long working day (fourteen or fifteen hours in winter) and an inadequate wage (four or five marks for a week's work is the normal rate for shuttle-weavers), with the disastrous effects of malnutrition and a depressing environment. The weaver works, lives and sleeps in the same room that his wife uses for the kitchen. Furthermore, although weaving is an industry concentrated chiefly in the country, the rate of infant mortality is very high among the families engaged in the work. Insurance does not cover the workers against illness and injuries arising from their work. It is only since July 2, 1894, that insurance against disablement and old-age have been made obligatory for weavers, but the way in which instalments are paid more or less destroys the efficiency of such a scheme.

In the toy industry, he found that 'exploitation of child labour is a serious evil—most children work up to ten or twelve o'clock every night'. He remarked on the tragedy of children making delightful dolls which, in other conditions, they would have loved to make, whereas actually they were the produce of 'people who are slowly dying of hunger'.

It is unnecessary to dilate on this fact-finding of, happily, another age—at any rate so far as Western Europe is concerned. Its importance here lies in the way it exemplifies the working of Joseph Cardijn's mind from the start. Driven by his mystique, he first wanted to observe, to *see* for himself. *Judgment* was slow and careful. 'Can any absolute judgment be made either for or against work at home on these grounds alone? It would be wrong to suppose that it could. The whole problem is so complicated. There are numerous differences everywhere, both in the environment and in the occupations, in the employees, in the way in which payment is made, and in the needs which must be satisfied.' Obviously, for the moment there could be no question of *action*. That would develop slowly, and, once again, strictly in terms of more and more seeing and the living process of judging as the facts, the people, were encountered in his priestly work. 'See, Judge, Act'—the logic of Cardijn's mind from the first was to dominate the story of and activity of his movement.

After Germany, France. There a Catholic Workers' Movement was only emerging with some difficulty from a long tradition of aristocratic and employers' patronage of the workers in an endeavour to defend the Eldest Daughter of the Church from the ravages of secularism, laicism and anti-clericalism closely associated with Freemasonry and Semitism. As we know, it needed the pressure of Pope Leo XIII to awake French Catholicism from its romantic royalist dreams. But, as in Belgium, the turn of the century had witnessed the establishment of the first Christian Trade Unions, in which, however, clerical and employer influence was very strong. But behind rather tentative experiments in partial workers' autonomy, the pioneers were thinking hard and endeavouring to work out practical and satisfactory solutions to the problem of how French Catholics could safely, yet effectively, carry out Papal teaching in a hostile environment. The annual Semaine Sociale, or national week's social study conference, still today the French social highlight of the year, had begun as early as 1904, and Cardijn was impressed at this time when he attended the Semaine Sociale at Amiens. Only some sixty miles from Brussels lay the great French industrial region of Roubaix and Lille where the first Christian Trade Unions in the textile industries had been founded. Here was a rich field to explore. Pioneer of the fresh Catholic approach was the Abbé Six, who ran the review *La Démocratie Chrétienne*; so Cardijn consulted him. But the greatest impression on him was made by two outstanding men, Léon Harmel, the textile manufacturer of Val des Bois, who, in Michael Fogarty's words, 'takes his place alongside Cadbury and Seebohm Rowntree as one of the great pioneers of personnel management',[1] and Marc Sangnier, founder of the famous 'Sillon' (Furrow) movement and groups.

Marc Sangnier was only twenty-one when he gathered round him a number of friends vowed, like himself, to devote their lives to helping less fortunate youth, and founded the paper which gave its name to his movement. They felt, under his remarkable leadership, that the secret lay in the spiritual and educational formation of youth circles. These would equip themselves, religiously, morally and socially, as leaders of a formed and autonomous democracy. This democracy, in its turn, would feed, as it were, consciences and develop the personal responsibilities which should mark Christian political and social life in France. 'So long as we have monarchy in the factory,' he said, 'we cannot have the republic in society.' Under this impulse, the movement developed along many interconnected Christian paths, religious, family, educational, social, political. The Christian Democrat, thus formed, would be able to reform secular or neutral organisations from within, in the personalist (as opposed to individualist or collectivist) spirit of Christian sociology. It was a bold and astonishingly successful venture, owing an immense amount to its gifted and attractive founder, and it in fact trained many of France's most distinguished Catholic social figures of later years, including Abbé Guerin, the founder and chaplain of the French Y.C.W. But the 'personalism' of Marc Sangnier himself counted for so much in the movement that its relation to the Church became difficult and, not long

[1] *Christian Democracy in Western Europe*, p. 189.

after Cardijn saw Sangnier (Sangnier was by four years
the older man), the movement, as a Catholic movement,
was condemned.

Very different was the story of Léon Harmel and his
textile undertaking at Val des Bois in the Marne depart-
ment. Harmel was nearly eighty when Cardijn visited and
saw his work. Known to everyone as the 'bon Père',
Harmel had by 1875 established his works as 'The Workers
Christian Corporation of Val des Bois—a religious and
economic association with the employers and the workers'
families'. This far-seeing pioneer had unlimited belief in
'all that was legitimate in human freedom' and he was
prepared to trust to the utmost those who worked for and
with him, even when he was unable to persuade them that
his views and ideas were best for them. By 1893, he had
reached the point when his business was run in terms of
the following constitution:

> The factory council establishes a real co-operation of the
> workers in the professional and disciplinary direction of the
> factory. Its aim is to realise as between employers and workers
> an affectionate understanding based upon mutual confidence.
> The council is made up of ordinary elected workers who meet
> every fortnight. In the council room the workers are asked to
> give their views about every wage change, about disciplinary
> measures, about accidents, health regulations, apprenticeship
> and work itself. They represent their fellow workers in regard
> to all claims addressed to the employers. In it they study all
> reforms likely to ease the work and make it more profitable.
> The women workers have similar rights in the workshop
> council.

From the co-operative enterprise itself a whole host of
organisations, for training, health, mutual aid, saving,
insurance, funeral expenses, depended, and all in part
financed by a small levy on wages. This amazing enterprise, fifty years ahead of its times, was strongly backed by

the Archbishop of Rheims and the 'bon Père' could not see any reason why Catholic employers in large numbers should not imitate them. They did not—and perhaps not without reason, for Harmel himself was a saint and a genius, who could pull off impossibilities.

One of Harmel's sayings was: 'the good of the worker with the worker, by the worker, never without the worker and therefore obviously never in spite of the worker'. Those words have constantly been echoed by Cardijn, underlining the nature of the vocation of the Christian worker which must be 'with the working class, *by* the working class, *for* the working class' and we cannot doubt that, in spite of the complete difference between the work of Harmel, an employer, and the ideas for forming youth within the mind of the young priest, the latter was deeply impressed by the former's success in handing over so much responsibility to the workers, male and female, of Val des Bois.

Yet Harmel, far ahead of his times as he was, had followed a line which, in practice, could not be universally extended. Some instinct told Cardijn that the line of the future for Christians could not be the creation of perfectionist Catholic islands, but the spread into the world of the workers, through a workers' *élite*, of values, philosophy and technique that could be indefinitely extended. In this, the example of Marc Sangnier was closer to his own views. But the difference in this case lay between the attitude of Sangnier, a layman, and Cardijn, a priest. Sangnier, who began so young and without specific training, never tried to clarify his particular *mystique*. Inevitably he drifted into difficulties in his relations with the spiritual authority of the Church and the Church's developing social organisations. Cardijn, as a trained priest, not only realised the vital importance of the priest in his sacerdotal and apostolic role for the spiritual formation of youth leaders or, in the continental phrase, 'militants', but appreciated the necessity of fitting his social *mystique* into the Church's organisation from the start. In practice, Cardijn's way was by far the tougher, for his work, for many years, was to be carried out for the Church, yet for the most part in spite of his fellow-Catholics, clerical and lay; but where Sangnier failed after a brilliant start, Cardijn was to end brilliantly after a slow and very painful start.

In one way, England, rather than the Continent, turned out to be a more fruitful field for the young priest's fact-finding researches. England had never suffered from the division which existed on the Continent between the clericals and the anti-clericals, a division that created so many extra problems and difficulties in the working out of a Christian social organisation and action. Britain's social and labour movements were evolved, largely by trial and error, in a 'pure' state, unhampered by bitter religious and anti-religious rivalry—religious and ideological leaders offering their contributions on their merits in an undramatic atmosphere. In fact, that leadership within the Free Churches, the Church of England and the Catholic Church (where the name of Manning carried such weight through-out the country) had helped to realise a spirit of Christian democracy and Christian socialism that penetrated far deeper into the people than its more artificial, legalistic and combative Continental counterparts at the time. This was a practical and utilitarian atmosphere that strongly appealed to the hard-headed yet far from unromantic Fleming, Cardijn. It was as good as a retreat to meet British labour leaders, he said later.

In England he met such trade-union leaders as Tom Mann and Ben Tillett during the years of industrial stress and strikes when the trade-unions were fighting for political power within an ever wider and more tightly-knit industrial system. The way in which such leaders used new ideas, not for their revolutionary implications, as so often on the Continent, but as utilitarian tools in fashioning constitutional and democratic political power, obviously accorded with Cardijn's own views about the right way to promote his own apostolic, but practical and down-to-earth, ends. He delighted to find Tom Mann, a fiery Labour pioneer, expressing his whole-hearted admiration for a Catholic leader of the stamp of Cardinal Manning.

In him and Ben Tillett, who had taken a prominent part in the 1889 dock strike, which Manning had so dramatically helped to settle, he saw workers who had come from humble homes and, despite lives of underpayment, had managed to educate themselves, fitting themselves for first-class leadership in the workers' struggle on its merits, rather than as a means to gratify ambition or serve a dangerous ideological cause. What they could do, surely a formed Christian inspiration about the inherent dignity of man could inspire Catholic workers in Belgium and elsewhere to do for themselves. Not that the Belgian was content to see no more than a typical Englishman in Ben Tillett. There was more to him than that, and in an article written shortly after seeing him, Joseph Cardijn described what happened at their first meeting.

I must admit that I felt a little nervous when I rang the bell at 425 Mile End Road, the address of the General Secretary of the Dock, Wharf, Riverside & General Workers' Union. Ben Tillett had not yet returned, but I was told that he would not be very long as he had promised to see me. I was handed the *Morning Post* to help me pass the time. Suddenly the door-bell rang; the stairs creaked under a brisk step; and a man rather on the small side entered and held out both hands to me.

'Good-day, sorry to keep you waiting,' he said, and asked me to sit down. Exchanging his woollen coat for a light jacket, he himself sat in front of his typewriter and looked straight at me. Was it an illusion? No, it was there all right, the face of Napoleon, oval and full, profound and severe, the face of a leader of soldiers, the face that at this very moment was placarded all over London, announcing the play *A Royal Divorce*. The more I looked at him, at his gestures, his face, the more I was forced to admit that the resemblance was undeniable.

He asked me, rather defiantly, my name, my profession, the object of my stay in London, and finally concluded his interrogation with the words 'The Catholic Church is a clever Church. The Church of England would never send its priests to study the workers' organisations.' The ice was broken and we became the best of friends. I asked him question after question and he answered them all. He dug up all the documents relating to the movement to which he had devoted his life and which he directed so brilliantly. Finally, he bade me farewell, for he had much work to get through, and arranged a second meeting. 'You are a Belgian,' he said. 'I don't like Belgium. I was once a prisoner in Antwerp. No, I don't like Belgium.' He shaped his lips as though to spit out something distasteful. His awakened memory made him look to me like a brutal and capricious tyrant. I watched him closely. 'One last question, sir, are you English?' I asked. 'I am Irish but I have French blood in my veins and I have always lived in England.' I understood at once the extraordinary mixture of French enthusiasm, Irish joviality and English tenacity. I answered: 'I thought so. You don't look like an Englishman.' He smiled at this and I guessed the cause of his amusement. I ventured farther. 'Will you allow me to tell you whom you resemble?'—'Certainly.'—'Without wishing to flatter you, I would say you looked very like Napoleon.' He smiled, obviously pleased at this remark which must often have given him pleasure, stretched out his hand, 'Till Friday, then. Good-bye.'

In London, Cardijn found food for thought also at 'Speakers Corner' in Hyde Park. Here were self-educated people of all types, standing on soap-boxes, as he had done, and preaching their religious and political gospels. If *they* could do so, so could others—and to better purpose.

Another great Englishman whom Joseph Cardijn met was Baden-Powell, whose Boy Scouts had recently been founded, spreading not only in Britain but in many other countries with great rapidity. Its ideals, its organisation and its success greatly interested the schoolmaster of Basse-Wavre as well as the priest with his workers' youth mission. The interest was mutual, for the Chief Scout wanted to make Cardijn head of the scouts in Belgium.

Long ago I went to see Baden-Powell [Cardijn, then a Canon, said in a speech]. I spent several days with him in London when I was beginning in 1910. He said to me: 'Would you like to become head of Scouts in Belgium?' And I answered: 'Do you realise that the young workers—the young workers as such—have problems, problems quite peculiar to them?' Baden-Powell answered: 'I only know men—not young workers, whether boys or girls. I want to form men.'—'Do you know the way they have to live, these young workers, in that particular factory, in that particular working environment? How are they to be helped to exercise around them the right influence?'—'I don't know the working class environment.'—'But I do. I know that there are young workers, men and women. For me, that is the problem.' This is worth thinking about. I admire the Scout movement; but it cannot save the young workers nor the working class of the world. Yet, without that working class, the Church is lost. The same argument applies to other movements.

This conversation took place before Joseph Cardijn had ceased to be a schoolmaster and before he had had any opportunity even of experimenting with the special vocation he had at heart. It is evidence of the astonishing clearness with which he already saw the special line which he must take, despite his school work which, one would have thought, might have broadened his early call and experience and widened his conception of the youth question generally. In fact, his four years at Basse-Wavre were valuable to him because his bourgeois pupils were guinea-pigs on whom he tried out his ideas about how young people should be formed, how their interest must be aroused and held, how their confidence should be gained, how the latent idealism in the least hopeful among them could be drawn out. He never punished, but knew the way to coax the lazy and indifferent to make the required efforts.

Outside school hours and school terms, the Basse-Wavre region was also excellent for social field-work. This was Walloon country where anti-clericalism among the navvies and other manual workers was spreading. Around him lived, in fact, what he called the lost working class—the heart of the challenge that faced him. No wonder Joseph Cardijn would walk to near-by Waterloo and see in the great causes for which the battle was won and was lost a symbol of the battle which he had to win during his life-time. Meanwhile he would begin fighting the wider fight, speaking in the villages on the conditions of the workers and not forgetting his old campaign for the Flemish move-ment, linked as it was with the Christian cause. There was also work to do in persuading the local *curés* and *vicaires* of the spiritual importance of the workers' cause and the pro-motion of social reform, and the attitude of some of these may have been responsible for the later reminder 'Don't let them say he talks like a communist.'

All in all, we can easily form the picture of the school-master priest, pouring himself out in his original, enthu-siastic approach to his pupils, taking time off whenever he could to glean more facts about the lives and circumstances of his beloved workers; arguing with fellow masters and the local clergy, most of whom thought him an eccentric, and would have thought him a crank but for his gifts, his charm, the really unanswerable nature of his arguments; consecrating his own spiritual life to his formation as a future apostle within the Church he loved and revered as the essential means of training those young workers of the future to take responsibility themselves for their future destiny on earth as well as in heaven. And soon yet another turn of the wheel would take him another step forward, even though it looked as though the step was backwards.

3

A REVOLUTIONARY NEW CURATE
(1912–1914)

ONLY with difficulty can one imagine the Abbé Cardijn
remaining indefinitely a schoolmaster, but his success with
boys suggested that his fifth year at Basse-Wavre might
continue into a sixth, seventh and more. Instead, that fifth
year was cut short by a serious attack of pleurisy against
which his constant nervous expenditure of energy left him
with little power of resistance.

It was time to find another job, and while he was still in
bed in the spring of 1912 Fr. Van Engeland, a fellow master
in the school, told him that a new curate was needed in the
'royal' parish of Laeken in Brussels. He got out of bed with
a haste that suggests that even a royal parish powerfully
attracted his missionary zeal after the long years of preparation. He was appointed by the Cardinal. Within a few
days, on Maundy Thursday of that year, he presented himself to Fr. Coorman, the Dean of Laeken, at the presbytery.
The Dean, who was the friend and confessor of Leopold II,
was at dinner with many of the clergy of the deanery who
had come for the distribution of the holy oils. The new
curate knocked and entered the dining-room. The sight of
the young emaciated priest, coughing and still bearing all
the signs of his illness, infuriated the Dean. 'Look what
they've sent me,' he exclaimed to his guests. 'The Cardinal
can't have any idea of the needs of this parish. All my work
will come to nothing. What's the use of an invalid professor?' A rough welcome indeed, but it must be said on

behalf of the Dean that he very soon realised his mistake, and the parish priest and his new curate often had a good laugh together about the unfortunate introduction.

Though the parish included the royal palace and the great world of ladies and gentlemen connected with the court, ninety per cent. of its 15,000 souls were humble and ill-paid workers. Sweated industry of all kinds abounded, not least among the women and children. Ten hours a day, or fifteen when the demand was high, paid the wretched families better than hours consonant with a proper home life for mothers and for children. One can imagine the degradation of the husbands and sons, pouring out of the foundries, the tobacco works, the sweet factories, the printing shops, to find their wives and their small children desperately carrying on at home or in the workshops to earn the extra pittances which were needed to keep a home together. Less easily can one imagine today the fact that the bourgeois classes, many among them excellent in their religious observances and good works, accepted all this as a kind of law of nature. The two nations, the rich and the poor—that was how Providence had disposed the world, and, after all, many of these poor people had made good. The rich looked upon it as a matter of initiative, hard work, seizing one's opportunity, the practice of the virtues of thrift, abstemiousness, self-respect.

This conditioning of the well-to-do and the respectable to the two nations of rich and poor, and the lack of imagination that seems so incomprehensible today, were very soon being shown up by the thirty-year-old curate who lived with his ageing mother in the simplest possible way. They regarded themselves as belonging to the nation of the poor and of the workers, the priest son seeing in his mother one who had toiled as a servant girl and who, together with his father, had sacrificed everything to her family. Nor had he allowed the thirteen years of studies and teaching to raise him, in his social values, from the class of the poor to the clerical class. Going about his work, he naturally and instinctively met the poor and the workers on equal terms as human beings with himself. His priesthood and his education, so far from being a cause of patronising, merely added to the naturalness. The priesthood added a new dimension to his love and enabled him to give what only a priest can give. His training and social zeal made him genuinely interested in finding out, as was his way, every possible detail about conditions of work, conditions of home life, the social, moral and religious problems which his worker friends had to face.

A vivid memory of these days was brought out in 1936 in the course of a conference.

> I remember, when I was a curate, twenty-two or twenty-three years ago, how I visited the hospitals of Brussels. In them I saw the way those poor workers were treated, how their confessions had to be heard, how one had to help them in their last agony, the way they were abandoned, the heedlessness about the duty of letting their relations know of their death. I suffered greatly at seeing this immense distress of the working class.[1]

All this he saw and sought to deal with from within, as a comrade and friend, not from without, still less from above. Nor did he conceal the fact that he was determined to help his friends and the friends of his friends: the workers, however widely they might extend, beyond Laeken, beyond Brussels, even beyond Belgium. This priest who was the friend of navvies and crossing-sweepers, who was to be found at the factory gates always hoping to make a new friend, who loved to be at home within the gaunt rooms of the downtrodden, was giving a new meaning to the *soutane*—a personal welcome to it from many who had associated it

[1] *Godinne* (1936), p. 32.

only with the comfortable church over there and with their 'betters'; dislike and often fear on the part of those who smelt a revolutionary agitator in anyone who fraternised with the lower orders and laboured to see wages, conditions of work and standards of home-life raised, especially when it was a priest who was going out of his way to do it all.

Maxence van der Meersch in his novel, *Fishers of Men*, puts into the mouth of his hero a report of Cardijn address-ing a meeting in Roubaix.

> Cardijn told us how he got the idea of starting the Young Christian Workers, and how he had brought it into being. He was then an ordinary curate in a poor parish of Brussels. He mixed a lot with the working class, and saw how little they knew of Christ. He understood their life and their sufferings, to what depths they could descend—but also the greatness of which they were capable. He reminded us of the hard lot of the working-class women, our mothers and sisters. I can see him yet, turning towards the boxes and saying to the em-ployers who had come to hear him speak:
> 'You employers in this hall, would you allow your daughters to go to work in one of your own spinning mills?'
> He described the early days, the long spells of waiting round factory gates simply to pass the time of day with one of the working lads, to be seen by them, to get to know them and win them over, one, then two, then three. He recalled the anger and hostility that was roused against him, how the rich called him a Communist and the poor were suspicious of him through their hatred of the cassock and the priest, how even a section of the Church itself, the parish priests, canons, bishops had taken him for a visionary, a fool, a dangerous fellow who ought to be shut up, like a Don Bosco.[1]

But even this picture, perhaps slightly romanticised, does not touch the point that, for Cardijn, prayers, sympathy, smiles, courage are never enough. There was the practical study and hard work to be done—the tough backbone of

[1] *Fishers of Men*, by Maxence van der Meersch (John Miles), p. 40.

experiment and organised action which formed a continuous hard line, linking every experience and piercing a way forward towards the goal which he had set himself.

Not long after his arrival at Laeken the Dean put the new curate in charge of the Girls' Club which, with its male counterpart, was the only form of parish workers' organisation. The members were young people up to the age of twenty, with the majority in their early teens. In the main it was simply a 'keep them out of mischief' business with a savings bank and mutual insurance scheme. Even as a club for games, amusement and distraction, it cannot have been much of a catch, for in that large parish the girls' club, of which Cardijn was now in charge, only numbered thirty. The annual excitement was the Christmas play to which the grand ladies of Laeken condescended to come in order to show their interest in the poor.

Fr. Cardijn blew into these placid, stagnant waters like a tornado. For the first time in his life he found himself actually responsible for the souls and bodies of a few real workers—thirty girls with enough goodwill and interest to hang on to a little parish organisation which ran a Christmas play. Unhopeful material indeed. But in those thin, poorly-dressed, scatter-brained girls he saw the birth of a Christian revolution. At once he imported into the club a number of girls of the mettle for which he was looking, girls whom he had helped and with whom he had made friends on his rounds in the parish. Soon he had them all organised into a study-group in which not he, the knowledgeable curate, but they, the uneducated girls, ran the inquiries. It was for them to find out what they really stood for in the world of their working-life, its conditions, the effects it had on their fellow-workers, the remedies needed to improve matters. Before they could judge and act, they must see—and that at least they could do. He would doubtless set the ball rolling, but the study-circle was organised and run by the members with their own president and secretary. As he had foreseen, these girls hitherto content to be victims of their class or ready to escape from their harsh condition through distraction, amusement, sin, were transformed by respect, responsibility and autonomy into new creatures who soon rivalled their 'betters' in taking over the complex business of running a self-governing society. While the priest dramatically set before them the example of Christ, on whom the whole work depended and whom they were themselves to grow to understand in their studies at the meetings, he knew, as a hard-headed social worker, that the practical side of any self-respecting organisation was of the utmost importance. For example, poor as they might be, each must be ready and willing to pay for membership, for that payment was the token of a worker's independence and readiness for sacrifice. Thirty-six years later, Cardijn still spoke of 'the revolutionary value of that little subscription'.

That young worker, how much has he to spend on himself— how much a day, how much a week? We must start from there if we are to teach the value of the personal, free, voluntary act of subscription. I freely give a part of that money to the organisation, through love for my fellow workers, to help them and to help train them. You must be prepared to insist on it and to get it from each worker. Some people think that the emancipation of working youth simply depends on paid holidays, better wages and decent working conditions. No, it also means making sure that working youth itself makes the needed gesture, effort, personal sacrifice to work for its emancipation, to train itself, without always getting everything from others.[1]

Very soon he had these girls, whose numbers very rapidly increased in response to Cardijn's methods,

[1] *Le Jeune Travailleur devant la Vie* (1949), p. 18.

completely responsible for the finances, accounts and secre-
tarial work of their organisation.

It was not long before that first group of workers of
whom the abbé had charge sprouted out into a whole series
of young workers' associations—little trade-unions—grouped
according to jobs. No fewer than ten were born in a single
year.

Cardijn himself has told of that early enthusiasm:

> How well I remember those early meetings. We were
> positively suffocating. Windows and doors had to be kept
> open and even then the air was not fit to breathe. The
> president was magnificent. How she loved her trade union.
> I remember a little talk she gave at the Needlework Trade
> Union on 'her beloved trade union', and how everyone there,
> guests and members, were quite amazed by her. What keen-
> ness in that teeming little world of young girls, keen-eyed, often
> boyish in manner and swinging their hips, despite the poor
> clothes they wore. All types of women workers were re-
> presented, most of them coming from the worst streets in
> Laeken: laundrywomen, ironing-women, workers in the
> chocolate and cigarette factories, girls in the feather trade,
> the shoe-polish, the wood, the cardboard box, the jam,
> trades, nurses, messengers and many others.[1]

The Christmas show of the past had grown into concerts
and entertainments of real quality, and whereas, before, the
invited and honoured guests had come to help and con-
descend to the poor girls, they were now, to their amazement, confronted with girls of the same type, but perfectly
able to greet the visitors with polished speeches of welcome,
to show them to their places, to run the whole evening themselves from start to finish. On Sundays, this new feminine
life—for it truly was a kind of metamorphosis, accomplished
simply by Cardijn's respect for them and pride in the girls
—instead of hiding itself in the poor homes or gossiping

---

[1] *Jeunesse Syndicaliste*, July 1921.

in the streets, went off for excursions to nearby towns and countryside, widening all the time their knowledge and field of interest.

In these working girls, most of them aged between thirteen and sixteen, was inculcated the dignity and pride of being Christian women and the dignity and pride of being organised as workers in trade-unions which defended their professional honour and their rights, guaranteed their future and provided a standard and an authority which others would have to respect.

Within months the thirty-strong girls' club had become the Women's Christian Workers' League, numbering 1,000, with its own paper *La Prévoyance*, later to become *La Femme Belge*, which lasted until 1934.

When we learn about this extraordinary development we have to rub our eyes and force ourselves to remember that we are still in the year 1913, for today, over forty years later, few Christian parishes would be able to boast of a comparable organisation for the young women of the parish —an organisation inspired by the priest, but yet successfully merged into complete youth responsibility. We can imagine, therefore, the reactions it caused in those days. This young priest who seemed to have the force to turn the world upside down was an agitator, a revolutionary, a madman. The rich, the employers, did not see anything funny in finding themselves confronted with workers who did not need their kindly patronage and help (even clergy-help) and who were capable of thinking hard for themselves about their conditions of work and life. They mocked and said 'It cannot last, this idea of preparing young workers for life.'[1] The anti-clericals were furious and resorted, where they could, to petty persecution and worse. 'How they suffered for the J.O.C.', wrote Cardijn who, it will be noted, had already in effect founded the movement which, in its

[1] *La J.O.C. École de Vie*, p. 9.

essentials, would never change from that first experiment, 'in their working lives. They were dragged by their hairs; they were beaten up. They were martyrs. They were heroines.'[1]

The wonder is that he was allowed to carry on—that he himself had the courage to carry on. Later he said: 'I began in Laeken in 1912, with girl workers of twelve or thirteen. How often I was tempted to drop everything there and then, to give it up . But I used to say to myself: I must go ahead, I must start again, and when some gave up I did all I could to find new recruits to fill the gaps.'

The new curate had been officially put in charge of the girls, not the boys. Hence this feminine start, one, in fact, which was always to give his work a note of equality between the sexes against prevailing bourgeois and clerical opinion. As such, however, he had no official authority to do for the boys what he had been doing for the girls. Not surprisingly, however, some of the boys began to envy these self-sufficient girls who were being transformed by the young priest's fiery zeal and extraordinary attraction. 'What are you going to do for us?' they were asking him.

Among them was a boy of about eighteen, called Fernand Tonnet. He was a bank employee, and with a friend or two he called on the new curate and asked him to help them as he had helped the girls of the Needlework Union. Cardijn wanted nothing better, though officially he had no commission to take them on. Let them gather together a few more and come to his rooms where his mother and he would be at their service. As so constantly in this story, that call was providential—or shall we say that Cardijn was one of those men who seemed to invert the usual phrase. For him God proposed the opportunity and Cardijn disposed of it to the extent of never missing it and all that it promised. Fernand Tonnet, in a movement wherein the priest and the layman

[1] *Cardijn, Père de la J.O.C. Mondiale*, p. 10.

were each to have their allotted roles clearly distinguished,
dependent on one another and each really independent in
his sphere, was to be the lay counterpart to the priest—the
first of the three lay 'musketeers', with Paul Garcet and
Jacques Meert. But the men's movement had to start more
cerebrally than the women's, and it was in Cardijn's
rooms that of an evening Tonnet came to pass long hours
at work, burying himself in his host's library of theological
and sociological books and discussing his findings when the
abbé could spare the time. He was working out the implications of Cardijn's first message to him: 'Every young
worker is a human being, capable of and wanting to
develop, to read something of which he may be ignorant,
but which is special to him. That young man has within
him what he needs to reach it. But he must be shown how
to do so by every sort of means.'

To Tonnet we owe the fullest picture of the Cardijn of
those days.

> M. Abbé Cardijn [Tonnet wrote, thirty years later] was
> moved by an inexhaustible dynamic force. He had the gift of
> firing with his ideal those with whom he spoke or those who
> listened to him. If he realised that some were only half
> convinced, he would put before them, with a gripping
> eloquence fed by his excellent memory, the example of the
> men of action of the last century. In ten or fifteen minutes he
> could sum up a life, hand over to you a biography and ask you
> to follow in the footsteps of that person. He was always
> putting before those who listened to him the ideal of con-
> secrating themselves to the working class in order to defend,
> protect and educate it. And when he touched on this subject,
> he at once outlined a lively picture of the Franciscan spirit,
> for he believed that the twentieth century would find much
> inspiration in the spirit of St. Francis in reaction against a
> mounting demand for comfort, pleasure and pagan living.
> M. Cardijn never let his young study circle audiences go with
> no more than a general impression of apostolic work. He

gave them the necessary documentation, pointed out what social and religious studies they must tackle, got them the books they needed, and arranged a time for the next discussion. Everyone was caught by the incredible activity of that young curate.[1]

The second of the three 'musketeers', Paul Garcet, came into contact with Cardijn in a more directly spiritual manner, through The League of Pius X which Cardijn founded in 1913. The fact conveniently reminds us never to make the mistake of supposing that Cardijn was ever tempted by his social mission to forget or minimise its spiritual aspect. One of the subtlest aspects of Cardijn's vision lies precisely in his power to see and constantly underline the primacy of the spiritual *without* thereby ever weakening the importance and autonomy of the temporal, but rather enhancing it. To Cardijn, an agnostic, a Buddhist, an Anglican are as much part of his mission as a Catholic, and to any of these he can offer the ideals and programme of his worker renovation movement without altering or minimising it in the slightest. Yet seen from the other end, as it were, the movement had no meaning for him save from its source in Christ, in the fullest Catholic doctrinal teaching about Christ as lived by Cardijn himself, the most fervent of Catholics. Cardijn from the first seemed to foresee in his spirit the ever closer application of the spiritual and liturgical teaching of Catholic Christianity to the needs of the contemporary world which, in fact, has marked the pontificates of the three Piuses, the Xth, the XIth and the XIIth.

Instinctively, therefore, he had reacted with enthusiasm to Pius X's decree encouraging frequent Holy Communion and its early reception by children. By this decree, after centuries during which clerisy and laity had tended to become separated, and awe rather than love had grown to

[1] *La Vie de Fernand Tonnet*, by M. Fièvez, pp. 39-41.

mark the attitude of the people towards Christ (that Christ of the gospels, always accessible to the simple people of Galilee and most of all to the children), the sacramental Christ of the altar was given back by St. Pius X as the daily spiritual food of the faithful, rich and poor, learned and ignorant, old and young. Paul Garcet and The League of Pius X, with its new infusion of divine life in the young, were thus important milestones in the story of the Y.C.W.

Against any separation of religion from life, Cardijn would always raise his voice.

> For an immense number of Christians, religion is only a private affair, something apart from their daily work. It should be its spirit, its motive power, its transformer, its super-naturalisator. This is the purpose of religion, religion that ought always to be singing the *Gloria in Excelsis Deo*, a public confession of faith, a credo, a preface to the glory of the Trinity. Religion is a whole life which, like the host, should be consecrated to God. All this, so that through this life united with Christ *per ipsum, in ipso, cum ipso* all honour and glory may be given to him who reigns for ever and ever. And so it follows that Holy Communion, which too often ends the day's religious life, finds its proper place. It is an ever renewed stimulant and the means of attaining a complete transforming union. *Then* you may say '*Ite*', because you will be right, in proper shape, for your daily occupations. '*Ite, Missa Est.*' It is for you to make your day a continuing Mass.

So Cardijn explained it in 1933 at the Semaine Sociale of Rheims in the presence of the future Cardinal Suhard who was to do so much to bring a living religion to the people. And typically he applied his point to the workers' lives when he wrote words which the J.O.C. has never forgotten. 'Without work there is no altar-bread, no wine, no paten, no altar, no church, no religion.' This truth is not only true in the literal sense; it is true in the spiritual also.

'Without Christian hearths, without Christian families,
there can be no priests, no religions, no missionaries, no
apostles.'[1]

It is easy, then, to understand how, with these thoughts
building up in his mind, Cardijn had founded his League
of Pius X not just as another piety or sodality to console the
oppressed but as a vital spiritual factor in the apostolate of
the workers by Christian workers proud of being workers.
Soon he had recruited 900 members. 'This host you see, it
has been here twenty centuries to feed you, you the poor,
the workers, the labourers', he would preach to them,
stealing Marx's thunder and showing them that the work
and labour on which the Church and even its liturgy and
sacraments depend made them co-operators with all within
the Church and with all good men outside it in God's work
of creation and in the Incarnation. He scorned the idea that
working-class status was any lower in a Christian ideology
than the status of the rich and socially privileged. We all
agree today, but Cardijn was saying it long before the
professors had thought of it.

Thus the Young Christian Workers, in ideology and
practice, had come to life long before it was officially born.
There was no paper planning, no blueprint, no publicity,
no speeches, no blessings. It was the incarnation of an idea
and a prayer that existed only in the genius of a young
Belgian priest in his first years of active priestly work, an
idea which had been growing, developing, broadening
within him since his boyhood in Hal when he first saw
what factory work did to the bodies and souls of his own
boyhood friends. From then onwards every experience,
every opportunity was seized to broaden and deepen the
idea and to fit himself to realise it.

Cardijn would always remain like that—not a theorist,
not a paper planner, but a doer, an experimentalist, under

[1] *Ite, Missa Est* (1933), pp. 4–8.

the influence of a remarkably powerful constructive imagination with the power of illuminating a whole situation with a happy phrase. He was like the scientific pioneer who has a hunch and tries and tests long before he knows the answers, only in Cardijn's case the hunch was more like a vision, spiritual and temporal, which he knew he must turn into practical politics even in the face of almost universal criticism. Happily, his courage was, if anything, even stronger than his insight. And lest the necessarily factual narrative in these pages fails to give the reader the measure of the courage needed, it will be well to quote again from *Fishers of Men* and without fearing that the novelist's imagination has gone far beyond the truth.

One of the characters in the novel is encouraging his friend whose first experiences of hatred, mockery and cruelty at the hands of Catholics and anti-clericals have tempted him to throw his hand in.

> Yes, that is what I ought to have said to you: we're in this world to fight, and win, and hit hard, and take blows and insults, to be let down and stabbed, like Cardijn. You grumble because the job isn't there to hand, ready made. You think things aren't moving, do you? Look at Cardijn. You heard him say what he's had to put up with himself: treachery, wire-pulling, stabs in the back, fellows who couldn't understand him and who thought he was dotty. That wasn't what he expected when he started the J.O.C.; he had a right to expect something very different. Yet it didn't get him down, and he's carried on.[1]

For years, Cardijn had to be a fighter—a fighter not only against the enemies of Christianity (there was a virtual anti-Christian persecution in Walloon country) but alas, against his own conservative fellow-Catholics.

[1] *Fishers of Men*, p. 42.

4

J.O.C. BIRTH-PANGS AND TRIUMPH IN ROME

(1914–1925)

In the years 1913 and 1914 the old order of Europe was drawing to a close. Liberalism and democracy had succeeded the *ancien régime*, and they had given birth to socialism's protest against the economic servitude of the proletarianised masses who saw little hope in the new political and economic freedoms. Christians, too, were beginning to appreciate the paradox of popular misery and frustration in the midst of apparent emancipation and prosperity and, under the lead of the Popes, were being forced to see the true explanation of the world's trouble in the complete divorce between the spiritual vocation of man and secular society's refusal to acknowledge anyone but 'political' and 'economic' man. But it was a slow awakening within a Christian tradition wherein a divorce between Sunday Christianity and weekday secularism had come almost to be taken for granted. The growing appetites for prestige, power and the wealth that derives from them were drawing the nations into conflict, while the know-how of the Industrial Revolution, together with the close knitting-together of industrialised people under increasingly powerful governments, would mean that if it came to war, the amateurism of the past would now yield to a professional, industrialised world battle with the masses of the people exchanging industrial domination for military. The consequences of such a conflict were beyond any man's prediction, but they must usher in a new age.

In Belgium, traditionally the cockpit of Europe, there still was confidence. Her neutrality was guaranteed, not least by the Kaiser's Germany, and to the Belgians the Germans were close friends. To a Flemish Cardijn, who knew his Germany and appreciated the social progress that had been made there, it was an especially bitter blow when in August 1914 Germany tore up the 'scrap of paper' and, sweeping into the neutral country, were in possession of Brussels in a little over a fortnight.

With them came the apparent ruin of Cardijn's plans. An enemy-occupied country, young men in the army (Tonnet had joined up and was separated from his chief), the pressure of work in the factories, the Church's necessary preoccupation with all the troubles and sufferings which a modern war brings in its train, all these could leave little room for the development of a new Christian world of youth.

On the other hand, war and particularly the suffering under enemy occupation in war can bring a new realism. The care of youth, when youth is exposed to death on the fronts or becomes the victim of enemy deportations and is subject to the special dangers of an anarchic state of society, takes on a fresh urgency, and in 1915 Cardinal Mercier found in Cardijn just the man to take charge in Brussels of all the Catholic social work and to be chaplain of the Christian Trade Unions. Tonnet, from the front, wrote of the 'moral armour' with which he found himself protected thanks to what he had learnt from Cardijn. That 'moral armour', we may be sure, was the protection which Cardijn could give in those troubled times to the workers of the capital. Fearless himself and determined to remain cheerful and optimistic, he was able to defend the interests of those of whom he had charge and encourage them, while

E

also doing what he could to keep going what were now cells of his own movement.

Meanwhile, it fell on him in his official capacity to protect the rights of the Catholic workers as against the illegalities of the occupying Power. He did so publicly, denouncing with such fearless vigour the deportations of young Belgian workers to make shells in Germany that late in 1915 he was arrested. A squad of police knocked at the door of his house, where he lived alone with his mother, marched in and took him to the prison of Saint Gilles. It was much more of a shock to his ailing mother, who, as he said, 'became nearly mad with grief', than to him. On this occasion he was released after six months, in June 1916.

His second imprisonment was a different matter. The war was now nearing its end, and Cardijn as a patriot was doing what he could to help the country to victory. 'We had installed', Cardijn has written, 'an observation post in a house near the station. From it we could observe the movement of munition trains and send the information to the Allies. Alas, after a time we fell into a veritable trap. Unfortunately, I had written a letter and confided it to a woman messenger who was arrested. I was arrested too.'[1] This time the accusation was the capital one of spying, and had he been officially declared guilty he would have been shot. Happily—indeed providentially, as he said—the charge seems not to have been pressed, but he remained in prison for a year.

> From prison [Cardijn wrote] I went on directing the study circles which we were still running. In fact, I never had the opportunity of doing this better and with a fuller preparation. I arranged for food and linen to be brought to me from outside. A young worker girl brought a bag containing these regularly every week. I got the idea of making a little hole

[1] These facts I owe to Mgr. Cardijn and to *Cardijn, Père de la J.O.C. Mondiale*, from which quotations are taken.

in the lining of the bag. In these I inserted the sheets of paper rolled up tightly into needles. This postal service worked wonderfully for a year with the guards none the wiser. As I was always alone in my cell I was able to draw up the agendas of the study circles, inquiry questions and the rest. I also wrote articles on the right methods of the apostolate as adapted to save the working class. It was from these written notes, roughed out in this way, that I later wrote the Manual of the J.O.C.

In this way, he not only kept his study circles going, but gave information and directions to the National Aid Committee in their work of helping widows and wives separated from their deported husbands. Not for the first time in history—or the last—captivity was to prove to be the birth-pangs of a movement and its 'bible'.

Later, Cardijn was to say that his work came to nothing for the first thirteen years, and that its first failure was through the 1914-18 war. But it was only a superficial failure and, viewed more broadly, one may look upon the war as yet another of the providential turnings. To a personality like Cardijn's, ever active, ever observant, ever stimulated by danger and difficulty, these were rich formative years, nor was the continuity of his work severed. Moreover, the great break-up caused by the four years of war, and the sufferings endured by the people, inevitably created an entirely new post-war social situation, offering the priest, now thirty-six years old, new opportunities. The lands 'fit for heroes to live in' were to need spiritual heroes more than ever, and the years of the 'golden legend' of Cardijn's movement were preparing.

Cardijn emerged from the war his own master. He remained officially in charge of social work in Brussels, and because of the growing work and responsibility which the job entailed he was relieved of the curacy of Laeken. The distance he had travelled is shown by a fresh boldness in his approach. The stage of piecemeal experiment was passed. The time had come to found something like a colony-hive from which new colonies could in time swarm to establish themselves all over Belgium and from Belgium throughout the world. The first hive was established with the foundation of what he called the *Jeunesse Syndicaliste*, Trade Union Youth. The title was a good deal more ambitious than the reality, but the reality was to carry much farther than the title.

This time it was a new departure, not a transformation of something already in being, though the girls' Needlework Union was still carrying on. A few chosen and enthusiastic disciples of Cardijn—Tonnet, returned from the war; Paul Garcet, soon to leave his bank employment to work permanently for the cause; and, a little later, Jacques Meert, third of the musketeers—were grouped together, and with sufficient optimism to launch their own monthly paper, *La Jeunesse Syndicaliste* with a print figure of 300. By April 1920 there were forty members present for the first 'Study Day', which the young president opened with the words: 'I declare the session raised', to the roars of laughter of the audience.[1]

But this was no amateur business. At 19 rue Plétinckx, where the German Kolping Youth had been settled during the war, Cardijn, with his mother and the first secretariat of the movement, installed themselves. Its long sloping roof behind which were the attic offices gave it the name in the movement of the 'mansarde of the rue Plétinckx'. In the three musketeers, and in Fernand Tonnet especially, Cardijn had found personalities of his own stature. Here were the lay leaders, the 'militants', formed in Cardijn's spirit, obedient to his spiritual direction, but determined enough and capable enough of running autonomously a genuine lay movement. A false start at this stage could

[1] *Fernand Tonnet*, p. 99.

have ruined the future. Had the start in effect established a clerical movement, the Y.C.W. would have been just another Catholic movement, soon probably to be absorbed in the hierarchy of such movements. Had the lay leaders failed to understand the place of the Church and of the priest in such a movement, it would have caused the ship-wreck that Cardijn was so dramatically to avoid.

Marguerite Fièvez, in her life of Tonnet, has described the atmosphere of the rue Plétinckx.

> At nine o'clock in the morning, Fernand is at his desk for several hours' work, thinking things out, studying, dealing with the post. Earlier that morning he had crossed the door of 'Christian Work Centre'. For a long time he had been on his knees in the roughly adapted chapel, of which he was so proud, dedicating his day's work and that of those who worked with him. Several others who worked in the house were there with him. . . . Mme Cardijn herself never missed that early morning meeting. The abbé had just mounted the altar step. Here was the heart of the whole work. Here, with his young lay apostles, he obtained light and strength to face all the difficulties, all the problems. Often, Tonnet would be serving the Mass. Already his friends and he were daily communicants, for the Abbé Cardijn led them from the start towards a deep liturgical and sacramental life, the direct source of their apostolate. After Mass, breakfast in Mme Cardijn's kitchen. In an atmosphere of spontaneous friendliness, pulling one another's legs, Fernand would start the ball rolling about some social question or about the young workers' apostolate. The best of study circles developed at that daily meeting.[1]

Some people may find it hard to understand how such a group of young men, leading an intense spiritual life, could be as natural, spontaneous and gay as their fellows—harder still perhaps to imagine how they could have practical, alert, even combative minds of their own. At any rate, the

[1] Ibid., pp. 106–7.

example set by these pioneers, directly under Cardijn, has always marked his movement, and the enhanced, completely human personalities of its members have sprung once again from the delicate spiritual-temporal balance of the movement. It is a considerable weakness of van der Meersch's *Fishers of Men* that its Y.C.W. hero, Peter Mardyck, sounds, at any rate in the English translation, too much of a prig.

The spirit of the rue Plétinckx is brought out by a contemporary memory, quoted in Tonnet's biography:

> Naturally Fr. Cardijn was always being overwhelmed by requests. Someone would come to chat about a trade-union group; another about family difficulties; a third might be a young leader of the Needlework Union trying to save a friend. Apart from his hours of work, it was for him one uninterrupted daily procession in his simple director's office on the second floor. His young co-workers were beginning in the end to find the joke a bit too much when, with the meal ready, they had to wait for the abbé twenty or thirty minutes, or even longer. Fernand then joined forces with Mme Cardijn who, despite her endless patience, was happy enough to find someone to share her complaints. Decidedly, her son was going too far. The august secretary thought it was time to behave like a naughty boy. Feeling unable to go and tell Abbé Cardijn for the third time that dinner was ready, he began making a frightful racket next to the thin separating wall. Glasses, forks, kitchen utensils, anything he could lay his hands on, were banged together. One of the others energetically banged the cover of the pan or the door of the oven. At last, despairing of any peace, the abbé came along, looking a little worried but with a mischievous smile on his lips. Without a word they sat down to the table. He had understood.[1]

The enduring physical monument to those days must be the monthly *La Jeunesse Syndicaliste*, the first bound volume of which the Mgr. Cardijn of today will take down from

[1] *Fernand Tonnet* ,pp. 112–13.

his shelves and proudly show to an inquiring visitor, as though it were something infinitely precious. Of it he said in 1945, recalling the memory of Tonnet and Garcet: 'Then a tiny little paper, a rag full of misprints, very quickly became the link within which one can still find today the secret history—and how wonderful it was—of so many years of underground life, of catacomb existence for the young workers who, like the early Chrisians, dreamt of bringing back to Christ the whole working class.' [1]

A 'rag' full of misprints it may have been, but as one thumbs the volumes today one is amazed by the faith, almost the cocksureness, of the writers. Their point of departure was the admission that the very idea of trade-unions for young workers was as strange and frightening to their contemporaries as 'the famous monster of the Congo', but right away the vast pretensions of that monster are delineated:

> What do we want? We want our young brothers no longer to feel abandoned to themselves in their choice of a life's work, career, office, and exposed to the deepest disillusions and the worst mistakes. We want professional secretarial organisations to advise them about that choice on which all will depend. We want them to be able to learn their job seriously, to be protected from overwork and exploitation. We want courses of theoretical instruction after their practical apprenticeship so that they may become skilled workers who, in enriching their country, will receive the full rightful reward of their labours. They must be respected in their health, their dignity, their virtue, their youth, their sex life. Above all we want our future married partners, the wives and the mothers of the working class, not to be exposed to moral degradation, debauchery and prostitution. We want our working youth to become more Christian, hence more moral, more chaste, more worthy.

The practical programme of these young men included the

Ibid., p. 100.

defence of the interests and rights of young workers; proper apprenticeship and professional training for them; organisations for finding them the job suited to them; fair wages; proper homes; decent and healthy working conditions; moral protection; unemployment and strike funds.

Cardijn himself, writing at this time on pre-trade-unions for young workers, must have sounded as though he was dreaming fantastic dreams:

The pre-trade-union must be a school of duty, a school, freely chosen and even desired as a privilege. It must be the natural continuation of the primary school—a centre of boundless joy, of strengthening relaxations and pleasant distractions, a nucleus of affection and strong friendship. My personal advice is that we must advocate the fullest autonomy possible, while bearing in mind the necessary authority of the big trade-union. We are only at the start of the movement. I dream of a great federation of apprentices and I should like to be present at a national apprentices' congress. I can see in my imagination all the preparations, all the details, all the conclusions. During the first two days only the apprentices will speak, expound their views and discuss. At the end of the second day, two or three social secretaries will draw up conclusions and reports. During these days, those present would include delegates from works, writers, journalists, representatives of the government. They are there not to speak, but to listen and observe. On the third day, the congress would bring together the apprentices and the senior workers themselves. The conclusions would be discussed; observations would be exchanged and new inquiries started.

All this, I am certain, would ensure the conversion of the doubting Thomases. There are so many things which the world thinks impossible. The force of the good, properly organised, has yet to give the results that one may justifiably expect. I foresee a kind of professional 'third-order', preached and organised by new *poverellos* of Assisi. We need more boldness to make the world happy. We must allow ourselves to be overcome by that holy wrath which sometimes seized our

Saviour before the abuses and hypocrisies of his contemporaries.[1]

Here was a rare instance of Cardijn unbottling some of
the pent-up force within him, a force which, normally, was
admirably canalised for practical results. But his words
give us an idea of the power-house within him on whose
fire he has drawn for nearly sixty years.

The work at the rue Plétinckx was quietly bearing fruit.
The Cardijn Youth Trade Union had established (1920) a
group in Antwerp; later it spread through Brussels to
Liège and Namur, in Charleroi and around Tournai, thence
into most of the industrial regions of the heart of Belgium.
The groups were federated, and all followed the same
plan of action, with the weekly Study Circle, in which
members took in turn the offices of president and secretary
and the different activities, such as starting and helping
the local sections. General Study Days and days of spiritual recollection were organised four times a year. This
establishment and progress had become, in fact, so solid
and effective that the great crisis of the whole movement
was rapidly approaching.

What was this new movement of working-class youth,
run by a queer young priest with a strange reputation who
had somehow got into the good books of the Cardinal?
Was it not sporting red, the revolutionary colour? Such
men, such movements, were dangerous in those days when
the socialists were forging ahead among the organised
workers at the expense of the Catholics. Was it not using
the badge of the golden wheatsheaf, the emblem of the
official A.C.J.B., the Catholic Association of Belgian
Youth, and using with it these new letters J.O.C.? Was it
healthy that there should be this suspect infiltration into
a movement that enlisted the best of upper-class college

[1] *Jeunesse Syndicaliste* (1920).

youth of Belgium? What would become of the parishes, if the young workers were drawn away from them by this new sectionalising? The young people were following Cardijn and disregarding the priests appointed to look after them. More and more questions were being asked and the possibilities seemed ever darker to clergy, employers and upper-classes, many of whom in their hearts were terrified of the working class and what it might do to them one day. And here was a Catholic priest actually *encouraging* the workers, even Catholic workers, to become as good as their betters, to educate themselves, to imitate the socialists, to seize power.[1]

Much of this criticism was ill-willed, obscurantist and superficial. Cardijn himself, for example, had no difficulty at all the following year at a liturgical week in Louvain in answering the objections to the J.O.C. on grounds of weakening parish solidarity. He explained how in many industrial districts the people when asked about their parish would answer: 'The parish, the parish church, the parish priest, that's where you go for baptism, for the children's first communions, for marriage and for burial.' And addressing the priests, he boldly asked them how many understood or bothered about the young workers of the parish.

Who understands their life, their conversation, their habits; the dangers to which they are exposed, the abuses of which they are the victims; the temptations, the scandals, the promiscuities among which they work and live, in the trams and trains on their way to work, in the office, the workshop, the factory, the mine; when work is over, during their leisure hours, their recreations? Is the parish interested in these young wage-earning parishioners? Have their numbers been

[1] There is no need to blame the critics of the Cardijn movement in 1924. The present writer on informing a family in Belgian society that he was writing a book on Cardijn and the J.O.C. was met with shocked surprise and reminded that the movement was not liked and dangerous.

counted? Has anyone bothered to train them for their worker lives? Have they been called together during their last year at school so as to give them a moral and special social forma- tion necessary for them in facing the life before them? Has anyone helped to choose their job and their employer? Who has bothered to get them together the day before they start work to show interest in this new, vitally important, stage of their life? Has a Mass been celebrated for their intention? Have the other parishioners been stimulated to take a part in such a solemn ceremony? Has anyone bothered to introduce these young people to older people in the same way of life so that, like angel guardians, these can help them in their first steps along the apprenticeship of this road of freedom? Who helps and advises them in the only too frequent cases when it is impossible for them to get out of their troubles alone; who helps in their professional training and apprenticeship, in moral guidance, in ensuring working cleanliness and hygiene, in the case of accidents and in all those conditions of work which have such an enormous influence on their health, their future, their religious and parochial life? And when they return from work of an evening or on Sundays, who is interested to afford them normal ways of improving their education, of helping them to pass the time and amuse them- selves? Does anyone help them to save their money, to make them foresee the future, to direct their steps, properly and fully, towards their founding a Christian family?[1]

In the light of such a plain-spoken challenge, it was not difficult for Cardijn to demonstrate the need and value within the parish of a Young Christian Workers section which, in helping to do all this, would help build up that true sense of community among all its members which a parish should possess.

But among all the criticisms and problems there was a technical one which could not be so easily brushed aside. The Church in Belgium very naturally required that its

[1] From *La J.O.C. et la Paroisse* (1925). Cardijn's questionnaire is still relevant and searching today.

different social works should be organised together for effectiveness and mutual aid. It seemed natural that the Young Christian Workers should be affiliated as a section to the Catholic Association of Belgian Youth, yet how little in common there was between this new militant organisation of young workers with a trade-union and working-class background and the association which grouped together for the most part bourgeois youth, not so much with any missionary purpose as for the Christian and spiritual protection of its members against the dangers of the world! Socially and in their aims and techniques, the two were worlds apart.

This became obvious at the annual Congress of the Catholic Association of Belgian Youth in Charleroi in the summer of 1924. Within the Congress appeared this awkward minority movement, two hundred strong within the ranks of twelve hundred Congress members. And they had their great moment when for three hours they held their sectional meeting—flame and fire bursting out within the gentle, comforting heat of the Association's normal routine. This led to the adoption in the presence of fifty-six priests, in Brussels on 20 July 1924 of the principles of Working Youth.

Once more, the very success of the new movement became its greatest danger. Many were converted and made enthusiastic by the evidence of the life and fervour of these young men who did not seem to fear turning the world itself upside down for their Christian ideal. Cardijn gave the order: 'Let us work! Let us not talk! Let us march forward!'

Alas, it was too good to be true. Complaints and representations poured in on Cardinal Mercier. The devil of fear had taken hold of those whose worst nightmare was a world turned upside down. Trained and conditioned to keep the wheels running at a comfortable pace, for the

Church which is eternal always moves slowly and cautiously, many of the clergy wanted to condemn this idealistic early Christian holy zeal, this awkward return to the spirit of St. Francis. They shared, too, the more solid apprehensions of the upper and employing classes who could see in it nothing but a highly dangerous Catholic socialism, doing, however good its intentions, the devil's work in disturbing the so conveniently established social and class order.

Cardinal Mercier, a saintly and enlightened man who had a deep regard for the Abbé Cardijn, was not easily shaken. But he also was puzzled by the spirit and success of this revolutionary zeal. Nor can the spiritual leader of a people easily flout the mounting evidence of what his advisers and his people think. He felt he had no choice but to condemn the new movement.

He called Cardijn to him and told him of his decision. It was the most terrible moment of Cardijn's life. His thirteen years' work since the first days of Laeken; all that he could remember of his life and his vow to his parents to dedicate himself to the cause of the workers; his years of training and his ever clearer, more defined vision of the modern apostolate of the worker by the Christianly-trained worker; his deep-seated *mystique* to save the workers, the masses, the paganised peoples for Christ by teaching them to become men and women as God created them to be, responsible, worthy, free—all this was crashing to the ground before him under the gentle, puzzled eyes of a saintly cardinal. There was only one last court of appeal left—the one to which in the last resort, and given sufficient determination, every Catholic can turn: the Holy Father.

He told the Cardinal he would like to go to Rome and see Pope Pius XI. The Cardinal not only approved this last attempt of his to save his life's work, but gave him a letter of introduction.

It was Holy Year. It was in Lent. At times like these even men of distinction in Church and State do not find it easy to obtain a private audience with the Pope. Outside Belgium, where a few were ready to live and die for the cause which was his life, but where, as he said himself, most of those who had heard of him thought him a danger at worst, a figure of fun at best, the Abbé Cardijn was a simple and unknown priest. He had never travelled so far as Italy and Rome and he was totally ignorant of the etiquette of the Vatican. He knew no one with power to obtain a private audience in the rush of seasonal requests for such audiences. He even had the wrong clothes.

As he turned about for help in the Eternal City, with its vast numbers of Holy Year pilgrims, he was greeted with pitying smiles. There was no chance whatever of an ordinary priest like him being received by the Pope at such a time. The best he could do was to try to squeeze in at a public audience. The opportunity came. 'Get in the second row,' he was told, 'the Pope will pass by and give you his blessing, you and the others. You will be able to return to Belgium and say that the Pope has blessed you and your work.'

This, not surprisingly, was not good enough. His own account is 'I wanted to be received in private audience. My wish at last was granted. I managed to work my way, almost to filter my way along, from room to room. And suddenly I found myself beside the Holy Father.'

Pius XI was greatly astonished to see this excited priest with the wrong clothes unexpectedly appearing in his study.

'What do you want?' he asked, wondering doubtless how this man had managed to evade those responsible for the privacy of the Holy Father. Face to face with the Pope, Cardijn was terrified. But through his stutters he managed to blurt out 'Most Holy Father, I want to kill myself in

order to save the working masses.' One would have thought
that any premonitions the Pope might have had that some
dangerous lunatic had appeared would have been immediately confirmed. Instead, Pius XI looked at him and
answered at once:

> At last! Here is someone who talks to me of the masses, of
> saving the masses. Everyone else talks to me of the *élite*.
> What is needed is an *élite* in the masses, the leaven in the paste.
> The greatest work you can possibly do for the Church is to
> restore to the Church the working masses which she has lost.
> The masses need the Church and the Church needs the masses.
> Yes, indeed, the Church in accomplishing her mission greatly
> needs the working-class masses. A Church in which only the
> well-off are to be found is no longer our Lord's Church. Our
> Lord founded the Church mainly for the poor. That is why it
> is necessary to restore to him the working masses.

The unofficial and unscheduled audience lasted an hour.
When the unknown priest, condemned in his own country,
had explained to Pius XI the nature and purpose of his
work, the Papal answer was: 'Not only do we bless your
movement, we want it. We make it ours. I will have your
Cardinal informed of all this.' [1] And Cardijn, in very
different circumstances, was to return every year to Rome
to keep the Pope personally informed of the progress of the
Young Christian Workers.

It was a truly remarkable episode: decision to condemn
in Belgium; almost miraculous access to the Pope in such a
year and at such a time; the Pope's wholehearted welcome
and his by-passing of the normal channels to throw his
whole weight behind the work of a simple priest. The
Pope's almost uncritical acceptance of a priest who had
been so much opposed by clericals and bourgeoisie in his
own country is all the more astonishing in that Pius XI

---

[1] *Cardijn, Père de la J.O.C. Mondiale*, pp. 16, 17, and Mgr. Cardijn's personal
account to the writer of this decisive visit to Pope Pius XI.

was by temperament a rugged conservative, personally much preoccupied by the very dangers, socialism and communism, which in Belgium had caused Cardijn's movement to be mistrusted.

In accepting the natural explanation of something virtually unprecedented, we must also accept, apart from astonishing luck, Cardijn's own personality and his power to find expression for the spiritual fire and flame within him. The thirteen years of failure were ended. With such backing, nothing now could stop the march forward of Joseph Cardijn and his disciples.

5

THE Y.C.W.'s 'BIBLE'

(1925)

THE sounding of the Papal all-clear was followed by
Cardinal Mercier's formal approval of the Young Christian
Workers in Belgium. This deliverance did not mean that
the organisation could at last get down to serious work;
nor did it mean that everyone would approve it and smile
on it. It had begun its serious work a long time before and
its many critics were still free to say what they thought
about it, but they could no longer hope to check its rapid
progress. And rapid progress was now made possible by
official approval.

Cardijn, his three musketeers and the other leaders, to
the amazement of many who still looked upon the movement as unstable mushroom growth, concentrated on the
complex and formidable task of immediately launching the
first National Congress of the Young Christian Workers in
Brussels.

It is easy to say this, as of any national congress. But one
needs a touch of imagination to appreciate what it meant
to young and often inexperienced men working in virgin
soil and wondering all the time whether their frantic
efforts would prove a complete flop, as many people thought
likely, or whether their movement would be launched in a
grand and impressive way, the precursor of many a congress
and rally as the Y.C.W. spread throughout their own country and across Belgium's frontiers to the world.

Hopes ran high, but fears could not be wholly repressed.

Cardijn himself—not a person who thought that public display could replace the hard, unsung work of organisation and steady progress, however tentative and humble, —always realised, nevertheless, the vital moral force of demonstrations, meetings, enthusiasms, as heartening the members of the movement and as publicity for it. He had from early years appreciated the value of the public platform and of dramatic entertainments. Certainly one side of his nature was near to that of a showman in the Continental tradition, and not very readily appreciated in Anglo-Saxon countries.

At last the great day was on them: Holy Saturday, 18 April 1925. At a quarter to six that evening, all the organising work was crowned by the sight of nearly 150 delegates, only a fraction of the numbers that could be expected for the morrow, Easter Sunday. Their fears were over.

On Easter Sunday those present numbered over four hundred, four hundred young Belgian Catholic Workers who could wire their homage to the Pope and to the King. Cardijn, officially the chaplain-general of the movement, introduced the general programme, and it is worth underlining the points which he made at this official inauguration of his life's work.[1]

Our programme [he insisted] is not a proclamation flung at the socialists[2] and the communists. It is not a negative programme, but very much a positive one—for positive claims. We must be able tomorrow to say of our programme that it is the finest, the grandest of all, that it is the most striking manifesto in defence of the rights of young workers. The J.O.C. is not the same sort of thing, as some believe, as a federation of patronages, of athletics, of dramatics. No! The

[1] Quotations are from the *Manuel de la J.O.C.*

[2] British readers should remember that 'socialism' in the then context of Belgium was an anti-Christian, fully Marxist, socialism.

J.O.C. is social grouping which must help in the serious and
regular organisation of our society.

Again and again he insisted on this concrete and constructive social purpose which had to be achieved together
with other workers' organisations, and he came back to the
accusation made against them of showing socialistic trends.

> We are not interested in the socialist party nor in com-
> munism; we are interested in the soul and the destiny of our
> young workers. If these souls are to spread their wings, their
> rightful claims must be slowly, methodically, but ener-
> getically, pursued. Their soul, indeed, is not separate from
> their bodies; their spiritual life from their lives as workers.
> For us the soul of a boy or girl apprentice is worth as much as
> the soul of the child of a millionaire.

And the speaker, in the words of the report, 'then summarised in a succinct manner all the articles [of the Con-
gress] relating to stability of employment, to apprenticeship and professional teaching, to security of work, to
hygiene and cleanliness, to decency at work, to hours of
working, to night work and Sunday work, to heavy and
dangerous work, to the wages of adolescents and to the
situation of young employees'.

Towards the end, he insisted again on the fact that the
J.O.C. was not interested in theory only. 'If we have
already found leaders and apostles, it is not only because
we have Study Circles, but because we have put this *élite* at
the service of the masses. It is necessary to learn to act. We
must give responsibility to the members of our sections of
the J.O.C. from their youngest years.' Nor did he forget
his first love, the young worker girls, already the Jeunesse
Ouvrière Chrétienne Feminine, 'our wives, our mothers, of
tomorrow'.

Doubtless, after all this, the delegates were ready for the
lunch which in the report is delightfully described in these

words: 'The greatest animation reigned in the dining-room. The tables had been covered with floral decoration in the best taste, the democratic silver with its sober high-lights harmonising with the brilliant glitter of the glasses. Flowers on all the tables and, around the tables and the flowers, discreet young girls buried in their vast aprons were busily moving about.'

The now very rare first publication of the movement, the *Manuel de la J.O.C.*, contains a report of the first National Congress, but this 'bible' of the Cardijn revelation also shows that there was something much more important than the Congress, namely the practical spirit and wide scope of what had already been created behind the scenes.

The greater part of the *Manuel* contained, in fact, in well over a hundred pages, the general programme of the J.O.C., as composed by Cardijn himself from those reflections and notes on which he had worked in his cell during the months of his second imprisonment. Here was the hard reality behind the show, and anyone who reads those pages today cannot but be impressed by the amount of imaginative and hard practical thinking that made them possible. They represent the solid fruits of those years when the student and the young priest kept his eyes always open, all the time seeing into and judging every nook and cranny of the religious and social scene around him in Brussels and on his travels. In essence, the programme of the *Manuel* has never been changed, though the clarity of the Cardijn vision has always allowed for great flexibility in its application. It can be said also that in those pages lie the basic principles of all forms of effective contemporary Christian missionary and apostolic work in so far as these derive from and depend upon the authority of the Church. Unwittingly, Cardijn was pioneering far more than his own movement, as we shall see. In the way the programme is written, too, are curiously reflected the mind, the character and the values of Cardijn, for in it there is a disconcerting, but vital mix-up of sweeping idealism and the homeliest, most detailed theory in a manner that must have greatly puzzled the remote priests and professors.

Divided, under many heads, into *les faits* and *les vôeux*, the programme analyses the contemporary state of things in the social order, contrasting it with the necessary changes that must be fought for by the movement. But the heart of it lies perhaps in Cardijn's exposition of the true method of making responsible Christian men out of the material of the day:

There is only one truly effective educational method fully adapted to the age, the mentality, the needs of young wage earners. It is that of their *special* organisation, in which, *with them, by them and for them,* it is they themselves who work at their proper formation and little by little come to take the initiative in the practice of responsibility, devotion, generosity and brotherly co-operation. In their organisation they learn freely to accept necessary discipline, to exercise their own authority over their fellow workers; they come to realise their duties and their rights. Thus they derive a true idea of their dignity and their worth. Thus they develop a concrete professional conscience in discussing together the day-by-day conditions of their work and their lives. Thus they prepare themselves for their future family and civic responsibilities by a loyal study of Catholic moral teaching, which makes clear to them the sublime implications of their need for affection, friendship and love, and which inculcates self-respect and respect for those who tomorrow will be their sweethearts and wives, capable and worthy of being the mothers and the educators of their children. . . .

The whole organisation of working youth with its secretariats, its meeting-rooms, its services of professional orientation, of savings, insurance, its trade-union sections, its study circles, its journals, its badge, its subscriptions, its committees and its congresses, together create a mentality and a point of view, a climate of ideas, which exercise an influence and a prestige, stimulate the imagination, create an atmosphere, a sense of emulation and, above all, a mass psychology, thanks to which the young workers have more confidence, acquire greater boldness, are more watchful about themselves while feeling themselves better protected, better understood and better loved.

Cardijn's mind and interests are reflected in the many points which he covers, though one can only give a sample. For example, he has not forgotten the white-collared young employee and, in terms more relevant perhaps today than ever, he writes:

There is much complaint about the position of young office employees. It is not because they wear dickeys and, maybe, cuffs or because their clothes are better looked after and they work in an office that we must see them as the aristocracy of the working world. Alas, how mistaken parents can be in preferring to see their sons quill-drivers rather than see them professionally trained. . . . Insufficient training is a frequent cause of black misery for young people who prefer soft to calloused hands.

Aesthetic education for the worker is not overlooked:

Do not imagine that this is a luxury and impossible to realise among the masses. Certainly, it is not the work of a day; but what wonderful results would derive from an integral raising of standards among working youth. All the artistic riches of our museums, of our monuments, all the beauties of our picturesque regions, the treasures of true literature and the joy of beautiful music are out of the range of our working youth whose eyes do not see and whose ears do not hear simply because nothing has been methodically done until now to create a taste for them among our young people.

Under moral education, Cardijn comes back to his key point: 'Experience proves that the most certain way of

saving young people is to teach them to save themselves.'
Morality is not just a matter of reward and punishment.

> It is not enough to tell them that they must avoid evil and do
> good. In the case of every action, of every course of conduct,
> whether at home, in the street, in the workshop, everywhere,
> we must show young workers, men and women, why such
> acts and behaviour are good or bad. The sanctions of eternity
> are not a sufficient reason. In each case, we must explain
> where exactly the evil or the good lies, where it conforms or
> does not conform with nature and human destiny; we must
> show the immediate consequences, physical and intellectual,
> of such an act and such behaviour. If we insist so strongly on
> explaining moral duties, this does not mean that the explana-
> tion of moral rights should take any lesser place in the moral
> formation of working youth. In practice, these two correla-
> tive notions—right and duty—must seem inseparable to all.

And Cardijn, whose tremendous expectations were never
based on any lack of realism about the difficulties of life,
showed how good moral standards depended on decent
conditions of living in every field.

> Moral formation cannot be separated from a training which,
> for lack of a better word, must be called education in *savoir-
> vivre*, in politeness, in social graces. Young workers must be
> encouraged to have better manners, to know how to live, to
> be more polite, to have an air of greater distinction. . . .
> Triviality, 'couldn't care less', coarseness, neglect about one's
> clothes, about bodily needs, in one's pleasures, all this should
> be rigorously fought against among working youth.

He inveighs once more against a purely negative formation, refuting false alternatives as not only 'ineffective and
insufficient, but nearly always positively harmful'.

> A negative criticism of socialism will never impress the work-
> ing mass. . . . Only if Catholic social teaching, only if Catholic
> social organisation seems to the workers a carrying-out, a

fuller realisation of integral Catholicity, a magnificent setting-up of the social Kingship of Christ, spreading more justice and charity in the world, will it cease to be possible to accuse Christian workers' organisations of dividing and weakening the working class. The Christian working movement will then be seen to be the social unfolding of Christianity. Then only will young workers want to make sacrifices for it. Then only shall we be able to number within the working class new martyrs and new apostles. We must give back to the young that pride, that joy in the possession of a fruitful truth with the ambition to spread Faith and Hope among their fellow workers. We do not remember often enough that workers have needed heroism to remain Christian. The ragging they have had, the insults they have suffered, have amounted to the hardest of persecutions. An intense social formation within a socially powerful organisation alone can inspire in the masses the necessary strength and perseverance.

These last paragraphs, in which the deep feelings of the writer can be felt, serve to remind us that all this was being written and done in 1925 not against a background of general indifference as today, but against a background of hatred and incomprehension. Cardijn's sentiments have often been repeated in sermons and books, but he pioneered them at a time when they were new and even dangerously disturbing.

The 'See, Judge, Act' which came to be almost the motto of the Y.C.W. does not seem to have been expressed in so many words at this period. Here we have instead: 'To learn to *judge*, to *know* and to *will* and because of this to perform *acts* and to acquire *habits* and *virtues*, and to further this education and this behaviour by means of an *organisation* which sustains, protects and frames, such is the one and only method whereby success can be guaranteed.' In effect it is exactly the same prescription as the 'See, Judge, Act' which has become world-famous. Likewise, the apostolate of 'like by like' fills these pages. 'Formation, merely based on words, books and hearing, on services and gestures, on practises imposed from without or repeated by rote; an organisation which is content to unite its members by subscriptions and material benefits; these will never form a working youth. Knowledge that has been lived, conduct consciously chosen, a living organisation, these three are nterdependent.'

Cardijn and the leaders had loyally accepted the incorporation of the movement with the Catholic Association of Belgian Youth, but observations like these show how strongly they felt that their movement belonged to a new and different world from the official organisations.

The Study Circle, especially for the leaders of the local sections of the Y.C.W., was a vital part of the formation given by the movement. But there are study circles and study circles, and nothing is easier in any Christian Action grouping than to suggest a study circle. It is an easy way of keeping people interested and occupied, and the delicate problem of actually doing anything very much about it can be more or less indefinitely postponed.

Cardijn had his reply thirty years ago:

There are so many false ideas about study circles for young workers, men and women. There are so many complaints about their lack of success. Why? *Because the study circle has been kept separate from the action and the organisation of the young workers.* There lies the capital error. The study circle does not exist for its own sake: its only meaning is in terms of action and organisation. The Apostle said: 'Faith without works is dead'. We must also declare that 'The study circle without works is a dead study circle.' The study circle is not just a teaching business. It communicates a faith, a faith enthusiastic for social, moral and religious action and organisation. Such faith is itself impossible, inoperative, without such action and organisation. . . . Young members of the study circle are not simply pupils who every so often come to hear the master's lesson. They are first, themselves, the living matter which they study because they themselves in their life and work personify all the problems of working youth. . . . It is they who co-operate in seeking, gathering together, bringing all that other matter, living and lived: the facts, the inquiries, the books, the conferences, the lessons. The young members of the study circle are the workers who must see, feel, touch; they must move about; they must talk and act both within and outside the study circle.

In the study circle you do not begin with abstract definitions about society, wages, work, trade unions. You do not explain the definition of each word in order to deduce from it all that it contains. No, a thousand times, no! You tell, and tell again, of experiences lived, of events, quite concretely, in a living fashion. Precise questions about the life and the work of young workers have to be asked: 'Where do you work? How did you take up that work? How often have you changed your job? How much do you make? How are you treated in the workshop? What do you hear, what do you see, when at work? In what state are the work rooms, the shops, the w.c.s?'. . . . Nothing is more flexible than a study circle. Through its members and by its spirit, it is and it remains in contact with the whole action and organisation of the workers' movement in the region. Little by little its members acquire a religious and social mentality. They learn to speak, to act, to direct, to organise, to command. Thus the study circle is the cradle of the action and the organisation which, bit by bit, will take in the whole working youth of a parish, a district, a region.

In all this, Cardijn was vividly reacting against the *a priorisms* which must have characterised so much of his Catholic training and experience, even in social questions, just as they characterised those with whom he had worked and studied and met. Necessary as it might be within the scholastic system of approach, it was sterile and dangerous by itself, because concentration of theory could become an excuse for avoidance of action and the risk which action always entails. This uncompromising breaking with the past where the very object of the training was concerned, namely apostolic and missionary action within the world, was another characteristic of Cardijn's pioneer mind—and one in which he has as yet been followed only with hesitation, though any development on a large scale of lay action within Christianity must make it the approach of the future. Inquiry, not theory, will predominate.

And perhaps we may end these extracts from the *Manuel* which bring out so well the real spirit of its author's work with the following resolution, among so many: 'The J.O.C. demands that paid holidays, given for two or three weeks, to all young wage-earning workers, preferably in the summer or the autumn, should be organised.'

Cardijn never feared to get down to the practical level and never feared to be far ahead of his times. Years later, he told his followers that pages 79 to 120 of the *Manuel* foresaw the whole list of needed labour reforms.

In the *Manuel* is also set out what might be called the anatomy and the physiology of the whole organisation, and this, in principle, has never changed.

At its head is the General Council, with the names of the Abbé Cardijn figuring as Chaplain-General, Tonnet as President, Meert as Secretary-General, and Garcet as Treasurer. The permanent administration is in the hands of the General Secretariat. At that time, of course, there was no International Secretariat. Among other services it rendered was the pleasantly 'dated' service of the 'Photoscope', an 'electrical apparatus which projects and magnifies images previously photographed on threads of cinematographical format. . . . The Photoscope replaces very advantageously the old magic-lanterns'. The Secretariat also has a 'central propaganda team' at the disposal of the organisation.

The movement is organised in Regional Federations of all the local sections, governed by elected delegates from the sections who form a Regional Council which chooses its Executive Committee. This Council, in its turn, elects delegates for the General Council. These Regional Federations are represented on the Catholic Association of Belgian Youth, but 'they remain in close relationships with the Christian worker's organisations of the region, especially with the trade unions and mutual insurance groups, and participate in general meetings and manifestations so as to promote the social formation of the Jocists and lead to their being active members of these organisations'. Clearly, the fruitful connection lay there.

On the ground-floor, below the staff work of 'the all-important Regional Councils' come the Local Sections of the J.O.C. Each section elects a committee from members of six months' standing, of whom the priest-director approves. Each section also forms a study circle for the training of leaders and for service on the committee. The leaders should be taken from manual workers as much as from brain workers. They are in fact what are called on the Continent 'militants', the dynamic force of the whole in spreading the movement by enlarging sections and opening new ones and by working for the movement's social demands. 'Let there be no mistake about it, the J.O.C. intends to organise both an *élite* and a *masse* among the young workers. The *élite* must be formed in the study circles, in the committee meetings and by personal relations in the work of fermenting the mass.'

At every level of the organisation there is a chaplain or priest-director, for the movement as a whole, for the Regional Federation, and for the Local Section. But it is important to underline both the importance of the priest and the limits of his importance. The priest is the spiritually formative element, the helping hand; he does not take the place of the lay leader or limit the latter's autonomy in the work and purpose of the movement.

Speaking eight years later at Rheims, Cardijn said:

The essential role of the chaplain is simply this: to furnish leaders. The J.O.C. is absolutely dependent on leaders. A section without a leader, a federation without a leader: neither can be the true J.O.C. Nor is it enough that there should be leaders capable of presenting demands, of doing good propaganda, even of penetrating within the working class. It is essential that they should become also true educators of their comrades and that they should therefore supernaturalise and transform their lives. Hence the need always to keep in contact with the masses. But if their action is to be effective, it must be limited to small numbers. Five members, ten members, at a time need a leader who can be interested in all aspects of their lives, who makes it his business to be so, who prays for them, who uses all the plans of the J.O.C., all its activities, all its services as the means of forming young workers.[1]

And in a classic passage in 1935 he described the full task of the chaplain:

Note well that there can be no local, regional or national leaders without the priest. The role of the priest in the J.O.C. is to be the one who holds in his hands, through his priestly character, doctrine, grace and the sacraments. Of these he must be the channel, the guardian. He must raise up leaders, furnish their weapons and train them, for these are the kernel of Jocism, its head, its heart without whom no conquest is possible. The priest will give them faith in conquest; if need be, he will make martyrs of them. He will give them, not only the spirit of conquest, but the guide to conquest.[2]

The general organisation of the movement, it will be seen, is a very practical combination of spiritual and social authoritarianism with genuine democratic delegation. Cardijn, as we have seen, did not think in terms of generalisations, labels and catchwords. His organisation was moulded

[1] *Ite, Missa Est*, p. 10.
[2] *Semaine d'Etudes Internationale* (1935), p. 155.

to the all-important purpose. He saw that the authoritarianism of the priest was both inherent in the Church and
essential to his plan. But the purpose of that authoritarianism was to enable the layman to take over responsibility and freedom in his proper field. It was Cardijn's deep
feeling for the Church which made him see the Church as
essentially missionary or apostolic. For him a 'Father' who
does not form Christian apostles within the world is barren.
Thus the apostolic, missionary priest who, through his
unique supernatural sacerdotal powers and through his
teaching and pastoral vocation, instinctively thinks of forming a spiritually and socially *aware* apostolic laity is at the
very heart of the whole Young Christian Worker movement,
as, of course, he should be at the heart of every Christian
lay movement.

Cardijn himself, as the priest who founded the movement and who has remained its chaplain-general, has been
called a 'damned autocrat'. It is improbable that he would
defend himself very strongly against the label. As the priest,
Cardijn *is* the Church's autocrat for the movement. By
mission and temperament Cardijn insists that his is the
right way, and he would not weaken his movement for the
sake of popularity or a democratic cliché. This realism of
his has imported another element of authoritarianism into
the movement, namely the all-important position of the
Leader who, first and foremost, must be the right man,
whether duly elected or not. But Cardijn's 'damned auto-
cracy' has also autocratically laid it down that his movement
would have no meaning unless the genuine autonomy of the
social and lay work of the movement—its very purpose, in
fact—is realised and safeguarded. In doing this, the 'damned
autocrat' has proved to be the least clerically autocratic
leader of Catholic lay movements. This lay autonomy and
responsibility in a pioneer movement, which, in fact, fell
somewhere between the Church's official Catholic action

and the normal lay Catholic autonomy within secular fields was 'democratically' unique within the Church at the time, but it has since been recognised by the Popes as 'an authentic form of Catholic Action', setting an example which, even now, has only been tentatively and nervously followed. The 'damned autocrat' is also therefore a 'damned liberal or democrat', just as the man who can inspire an extraordinary mixture of love and affection around him can sometimes also infuriate those with whom he works. The man, whose belief and trust in the judgment and decisions of others is at the very heart of his life's work, is not at all worried by the hero-worship and acclamation of his public rallies, where his picture may stand out on a giant poster with his followers chanting the cry of *Cardijn! Cardijn! Cardijn!* It is useless to try to fit into either time-honoured hagiographical characters or under reassuring political labels men with the vision, will and energy to make revolutions. What had been accomplished by Cardijn by the year 1925 was a revolution, albeit a revolution limited in its scope and in its impact by the straight and elevated path which he as a Catholic priest wanted to pursue; limited, too, by the fear and opposition with which he was met. But as a revolution in depth, in ideas, a revolution in the whole Christian and bourgeois apperception of the future of the worker and even of the lay role within the Christian Church, it had already deserved its historical place before its effects could be more than very locally realised.

Before leaving the *Manuel*, let us note one provision which may well be taken to underline as well as anything else the courage and boldness of its author.

It certainly will not be the case that all Jocists will at once join the Christian Trade Union. In some cases it will be necessary to create solid religious and social convictions. Then, obstacles in the Trade Union field which now seem insurmountable will be decisively overcome. Meanwhile, we must even allow some Jocists to be affiliated to the Socialist Trade Union, to the Trade Union called 'National' or 'Neutral', though, of course, they may not be propagandists for them.

A reader of these pages could not be wholly blamed for still seeing in Cardijn's Jocism yet another, if a rather more adventurous, extension of other edifying Church societies. And now we find Cardijn ready to admit that some of his pious Jocists will not have the courage or the requisite training to join the Christian Trade Union, buttress of essential Christian values in the work of industrial relations. More than this, he will tolerate his pious Jocists remaining in the enemy camp, for in those days, if not perhaps always in these, Continental socialism was universally regarded as the enemy.

What is the explanation? Surely it is that the heights of the Cardijn ideal set no lower limits for the intake of anyone, whatever he himself might be capable of, who could at least appreciate that ideal. There were no restrictions on entry to the upward road. But there was the greatest confidence that since the upward road was the right road, many who entered at the lowest level would achieve the climb—achieve it perhaps more quickly and securely than those who congratulated themselves on having entered at a more decent level. Later Cardijn would say: 'We must always begin by taking leaders as we find them. Let them be socialists; let them be communists. It matters little. . . . We should say "that is the type from which I can fashion a leader".'

A flood of light is thrown by this on the true spirit of the movement. We have grown used to thinking that ideals are only for the good and that any Christian society is open only to the good and *bien-pensants*. Hence the temptation to think of Jocism as another pious society. But Cardijn wanted not a pious society but a Christ-like one, one for the publicans and sinners and thieves whom Christ had come to save. It was up to them—not to a respectable selection committee.

In a different but parallel way, Jocism—born in Catholic Belgium and not excluding from its embrace the socialists and anti-clericals there—when it spreads to religiously divided countries is open to other than Catholics, whether they want to join Y.C.W. sections or whether another Communion, as has happened in Britain, wants to start a Y.C.W. movement of its own. Cardijn's movement, though uncompromising about its own fully Catholic path, presents a formula which, in itself, is completely unsectarian, in the sense that the individual non-Catholic can find a new self-realisation and an apostolate in its basic principles and in its social aims, while other denominations can use its methods for their own spiritual ends.[1]

A striking example of the impact of the *Manuel de la J.O.C.* is afforded by its effect on the author of *L'Action Catholique Specialisée*, Professor Pierre Bayart of Lille. In a letter to the present writer, Professor Bayart has told the story.

I had been invited by my bishop, Cardinal Liénart, in 1929, to study relationships between employers and trade-unions in the northern industrial regions of France. One day I was invited to speak on the subject to the Catholic Employers' Association of Lille, when, by chance, the postman brought me a parcel from someone who to this day remains unknown to me. It was the *Manuel of the J.O.C.* I interrupted my work to turn over its pages. Soon, I was reading it from start to

---

[1] The Jocist Movement, under the name of 'Christian Workers' Union', was started in Sheffield before the last war by the Rev. G. W. O. Addleshaw, now a Canon of York, who had met Cardijn and written a booklet *Jocism* (S.P.C.K.) which, to the knowledge of the present writer, Mgr. Cardijn greatly admires and describes as a faithful study of his movement. From Sheffield it spread to Iona under Canon Roseveare, S.S.M., and today it flourishes in Pallion, Sunderland. See *The Parish Church and the Young Worker*, by Rev. C. H. G. Hopkins, Vicar of St. Luke's, Pallion, and 'The Parish and the Worker' (*Christendom*, Sept. 1950).

G

finish. For me it was a shock and a revelation. In it I had
found all I needed for my lecture. Soon I was in Brussels and
calling on Mgr. Cardijn, finding myself in contact with the
living, incarnate J.O.C., in all its dynamism, in the very
person of the man who had conceived it in his brain and in
his heart. I had the key to all my own industrial problems
within the field entrusted to me by my bishop. I had but to
insert the key into the lock, in other words, to transpose to the
bourgeois and adult field a method which in the field of
working youth has proved itself to have a universal validity.

Instead of approaching the problem from the most delicate
angle, the social aspect itself, I understood that the real way
of approach must be from the spiritual aspect. Today I see
around me how far we have travelled, thanks to that method
of approach. In my own region of northern France we are
right ahead in the system of relationships on equal terms in
collective conventions, housing, apprenticeship, professional
formation, with the greater number of responsible posts held
and well-run by men who were trained in the Movement of
the Christian bourgeoisie.

Here then is a notable and concrete tribute to what a
prominent Catholic leader in social and industrial affairs
owed to Cardijn's timely inspiration in a field quite other
than Cardijn's own. Even where Professor Bayart writes of
'spiritual aspect' it is important to underline the fact that
for Cardijn the 'spiritual' must always be 'spiritual *in*
temporal'—the temporal being, as it were, an incarnated
spiritual, so that priorities, as between spiritual and temporal or ecclesiastical and lay, can easily be misunderstood
unless very carefully defined. The example underlines the
sense which any student of Cardijn's life and movement
must have about the apostolic and social universality of the
principles which Cardijn so largely pioneered.

6

Y.C.W., GODIN AND PRIEST-WORKERS
(1927–1950)

BETWEEN the great aspirations and the fine-sounding words of that first Congress and the realities of advance, man by man, section by section, there was a frightening gulf. It was a 'tough job', as Tonnet said. The Y.C.W. stood or fell, Cardijn had again and again insisted, by the formation of leaders from the working classes. Tonnet himself was an outstanding personality, a heaven-sent counterpart to Cardijn himself. He worked ceaselessly, making contacts, founding sections, organising regions. Meeting priests and pouring into them the Cardijn ideas about Christian self-formation or social distinction, he simply amazed them. The idea of forming apostles and missionaries from ordinary working men and women, hitherto regarded either as hostile, indifferent or just passively pious within the parish mass, was something completely new. They were unbelieving at first, but many, taken aback by the quality of the leaders themselves, and seeing with their own eyes what could be done by this totally new way of looking at men and women, grew enthusiastic. It was a conception which worked—worked so well, as we have seen, as even to cause fears of upsetting time-honoured parish ways.

The difficulty lay in the snowball character of the movement's advance. The rare enthusiasm and formation of these first Cardijn-trained men had to pass over to more and more fresh leaders without too much deterioration of quality. Thanks to a prodigious activity—and we need little imagination to see Cardijn himself, still by the way in charge of all Brussels youth work, covering the country, as he spoke, explained, taught, trained—the snowball grew hard and firm enough to keep up strength and quality and, above all, to maintain a toughness sufficient to withstand criticism from clergy, employers, old-time patronage-type Christian activities, whose fears were anything but allayed by the progress of these new and dangerous ways of imitating Christ's own apostolate of the fishermen of Galilee.

Within a year or two, it was a question of thousands, not just hundreds, at rallies and congresses from the four constituent bodies in Belgium which formed the Young Christian Workers' movement. Owing to the language separation the Belgian Y.C.W. divided itself into the French-speaking J.O.C. and the Flemish-speaking K.A.J. (Kristene Arbeiders Jeugd) under the single Secretariat-General in Brussels, and the movement prided itself on the fact that for once a language and race separation had drawn men into a common fraternity instead of dividing them. The spirit which animated the J.O.C. and the K.A.J. was a factor in uniting the Catholics of Belgium as a whole—another by-the-wayside fruit of Cardijn's lead and a portent of the future when the initiative of the working class could draw peoples and nations together, divided by the policies and ambitions of their 'betters'.

The third and fourth bodies were, of course, the J.O.C.F. and V.K.A.J., the women's branches (especially dear to Cardijn as he had started with girls, in whom he saw the reflection of his beloved mother) which had been developing along lines similar to the men's and were to hold their first Congress in 1927 with two thousand women attending them. The strict division between men and women, which has not been followed by all national Y.C.W.s, seems to have been an inevitable consequence of the Belgian tradition.

It would appear to the outsider not to be logically in keeping with the general spirit of Cardijn's teaching, but apparently conventions were such that the strict division was taken for granted and may have corresponded with Cardijn's own personal feelings, though not with the implications of his ideas. His writings return again and again to the question of what he calls *pudeur*, and it may be that those early shocks which he suffered from seeing the corruption of his own friends when they entered factories and workshops left a permanent imprint on his mind about the need at all costs to guard against temptations in this matter among his followers. The degree of separation between the sexes in the movement varies with different countries.

Thus by the middle twenties Cardijn's work was securely launched in his own country. It was, of course, of its essence very much of a minority movement. The mass could not progress ahead of the *élite* and the formation of the quality of *élite* which the movement absolutely needed, if it was not to fizzle out, could not be other than slow.

This slow progress of the Y.C.W. itself did not, however, affect the revolutionary nature of the apostolic method which was Cardijn's most valuable contribution to the modern Church. This would in time profoundly affect the Church and its apostolic organisations as a whole. But Cardijn may have been too optimistic in his vision of Christian working-class leaders reforming from within the whole working-class status. A great deal of his reformist programme in the social sphere was common ground with secular and even socialist reformers. The fact that the spirit and purpose were radically different and even the fact that secularist reformers had, in general, but the shallowest views about the true meaning and potentialities of human nature, about the primacy of the spiritual and moral, and about the importance of the family by comparison with class and collective, did not prevent the gradual realisation of many of Cardijn's actual reformist demands. But, as we shall see, if this was so in Europe, the movement in its progress across the face of the globe was to meet again and again social conditions considerably worse than those obtaining in Belgium after the First World War. In fact, the flexibility of the movement was such as to enable it to attune itself to any and every social condition, from the high-wage structure of America today to the most primitive social conditions in the worst of under-privileged countries.

More difficult to judge are the limitations which Cardijn imposed on the movement through confining it to the pre-marriage age-group. His own interest, as we have seen, was with youth, and he envisaged a youth movement for its own sake and a youth movement as a preparation for adult life—worker, family and life-long apostolate. In course of time, the age-limits were set lower (to include the so-called 'pre-Jocism' for the dangerous fifteen-plus years) and higher —up to thirty, thereby including the beginnings of marriage and family. The criticism has been made, however, that much of the Y.C.W. spirit and fervour are lost once ex-members settle down to marriage and middle-age life. The answer to this may be found in the fact that Cardijn was realistic enough to keep his movement within practical limits which he thoroughly understood. It was for others to adopt and adapt his methods for different ages and different types of Christian lay-folk. Cardijn will live not only in the Y.C.W. itself but in a whole new approach to lay action within the Church. The problem of ensuring the fullest continuity of Christian life and action in the Young Christian Worker as he moves from youth to middle-age has yet to be solved, however.

In fact, the number of members of the Y.C.W. increased steadily in Belgium so that within a few years of its official establishment they numbered about 80,000 with nearly 2,000 sections, a number which appears to have remained fairly steady. When one thinks of the almost complete neglect even in so Catholic a country as Belgium of the problems of Christian working-class youth and of the lack of interest in any positive Christian formation among lay people generally, let alone among workers, before Cardijn established his movement, the progress made was re-markable. And apart from the actual growth of the movement, one must reckon with the ever wider dissemina-tion, beyond the actual ranks of members, of Cardijn's revolutionary teaching, both in the apostolic field and in the Christianising of the increasingly determinant section of contemporary society, the working class. Its publicity—such as, for example, *Jeunesse Ouvrière* and the *Bulletin des Dirigeants*—achieved a vast circulation. It was not without significance that in this difficult period of launching and establishing the movement, the humble unknown priest of Belgium, himself from the least privileged of classes both in Church and in State, shook hands, as it were over the heads of the established order, with the Pope. Not only had Pius XI saved Cardijn and his movement, but he alone had welcomed it as the supreme need of the Church in modern times.

Inevitably, this Christian workers' revolution, as it may well be called, was making its impression beyond the frontiers of Belgium. It was France—a country far less truly Catholic than Belgium, but a country where the Church was faced by immense apostolic problems among the nominally Catholic masses—that was the first to look to Cardijn for inspiration and help.

There in the Clichy district of Paris, within the 'Red' belt as it was called, a tall, thin, young and very junior curate, called Guérin, was deeply puzzled about his priestly mission among young Catholic workers. Like Cardijn, his interest in social questions had been strong during the years of his ecclesiastical training and he sensed the Church's need to find ways and means of penetrating within the working masses. In fact, however, he, again like Cardijn, was expected to accomplish his apostolate through the traditional young people's club with parochial sports, gymnastics and dramatics. It was not good enough, and with the help of a friend, a member of the local section of the Confederation of Christian Trade Unions, he was planning the formation of a young workers' trade-union. But even this did not seem to answer the real apostolic yearning within him. Then he learnt of the Belgium Y.C.W. through a copy of the *Manuel*, and through reading the *Bulletin des Dirigeants*. And the first thing he learnt was that he had been mistaken in supposing that, because he had studied academically the history of the workers' movement, he really knew it. He wrote to Brussels to subscribe to the Y.C.W. publications, and from these he learnt the spirit and method of the movement. Dramatically, he tried the inquiry method on his trade-unionist friend and, for the first time, learnt the story of his life. To do so before had not occurred to him. And the story of his friend's life corresponded with the facts of working-class life laid bare in Belgium through the Cardijn insistence that you must build on the concrete, living realities, not on fine theories. The inquiry method was extended to other young Catholic workers, and it brought home the potentialities that lay within these young people he had been supposed to amuse and keep out of mischief.

Nervously, the junior curate of the parish wrote to the rue Plétinckx in Brussels, hardly daring to think that he might be importing the Y.C.W. into France, and certainly unaware of what that step would portend. But this little cry from Paris was like a trumpet call to Tonnet in Brussels. Bogged in the inevitable problems of making solid progress

in his own country, he saw a new dawn in the appeal for
help from France. The Y.C.W. would spread beyond his
native frontiers to conquer the world. Guérin had already
interested some of his fellow-priests in the Belgian movement, and by early 1927 when Cardijn and Tonnet
answered the call by travelling to Paris, the first beginnings
of the French Y.C.W. were visible and the little group was
trying out its first infant steps. The travellers at the Gare
du Nord were greeted by a few milliners' apprentices of the
French Y.C.W. The international Y.C.W. had also been
born.

In the next issue of the *Jeunesse Ouvrière*, Tonnet wrote:

> I am bidden to announce to the Jocists of Belgium the founda-
> tion of the J.O.C. in France. The hope of our first Congress of
> Brussels is now realised: there are Jocists in France. . . . Our
> comrades began in poverty, isolation and prayer. Yes, the
> J.O.C. is launched among the people of France, and we must
> establish without delay the *front unique* of prayer and action
> between them and us that our Lord may protect the first
> efforts of our young comrades of Clichy.[1]

And he was proud to report that the French Jocists had
already gained a workers' victory in successfully demanding
of their employer that the dangerous custom of replacing
belts on machinery while still running should cease.

As for Cardijn and Guérin, they became close friends and
collaborators. The latter has written:

> When the Abbé Cardijn spoke to us, he deeply touched our
> priestly hearts. I can still see him as he spoke to us, the first
> group-chaplains beginning their work in the Paris region—or
> at Rheims before Cardinal Luçon to priests from all over
> France gathered together in a Congress, and so often since. . . .
> After having so often chatted intimately with the Abbé
> Cardijn I have often thought of him at the Malines Seminary,
> deepening within himself the sense of the gift of God, the gift

[1] *Fernand Tonnet*, p. 65.

of him whom St. John calls Love and who, in Christ our Lord, calls upon us to share in his own life. I imagined him then thinking of his school friends who had become young workers —especially of those in whom he had seen, as a result of taking up their jobs, a thinning of their religious lives—and asking himself 'how those old friends of school-days were going to be able to share the divine life of our Lord Jesus Christ, their Saviour, in their own long lives as workers?' Was not the J.O.C. conceived at that time? . . . In 1926 we were all enriched by the vast experience of Abbé Cardijn and the Belgian J.O.C.[1]

Canon Guérin then underlines how he learnt from Cardijn the 'irreplacable role of the priest' in the world of today and in the Y.C.W.

In the ordinary way of things, if the laity of the workers' world reflects, reveals and proclaims Christ (for they are a people whom God has chosen for himself among the workers that they may be the first apostles of that world), this is due to the fact that the bishops have sent out priests who, by the grace of their state, resemble a channel along which the Holy Trinity through Christ, raises to the level of the divine the life of those workers and makes it apostolic. The priest alone could not achieve that formation . . . and the movement without the priest would be incapable of accomplishing its mission. It is the experience of our enrichment as priests within that J.O.C. type of apostolate which helps us to appreciate even more the grace of our ordination. That is the experience of the French chaplains and they all confess it. . . . How often I have talked in the most intimate terms with Mgr. Cardijn. How many times I have travelled to Brussels during these twenty years and for one reason only—to spend the day with him, to tell him of our joys and our difficulties. And each time I have left him with a heart filled with hope, that hope which is the hope of the Church itself in its knowledge that the Saviour is there within it so as to save and gather together

[1] *Notes de Pastorale Jociste*, Aug., Sept., 1956.

and bring into the very depths of the divine life redeemed humanity, as it passes through death to resurrection.[1]

The French J.O.C.'s emphasis, under the leadership of the ascetic Canon Guérin, of the spiritual and liturgical element in Cardijn's teaching has proved to be of special value. It is not that the Y.C.W.'s social reformist mission within the working class, so vitally important in the development and work of Cardijn, was secondary in itself. But it may fairly be said to have been the product in some measure of Cardijn's own special circumstances, upbringing, special interest and times. And it urgently needed to be undertaken by a fearless priest-pioneer like himself. For him, visionary and hard-headed practical Flemish priest, spiritual insight and vocation, youth and the workers were intimately linked together, and had this not been so the apostolic revolution which he initiated could hardly have been accomplished. In scholastic terminology, the 'form' had to be united with 'matter', if anything actual was to be accomplished at all. But matter changes while form remains. With the passing of years not only do the special problems of the working class change, but the relationship of the workers to other sections of the community alters. It is because of this that Cardijn's application of the spirit and methods of his movement to the situation of the 1920s is, of its nature, dated, and indeed it is a point which the movement has well realised so that, to take an extreme example, the practical problems of the Y.C.W. in an advanced country like America today are totally different from its problems in under-developed countries. But what remains constant throughout the changes of application in changing times and different countries is the spirit and the essential method of spiritual, moral and personal formation of the Christian man and woman in a secularist world.

[1] Ibid.

The full realisation of this, especially as regards spiritual formation, took place in France. In fact, important aspects of the great spiritual, missionary and liturgical movement in contemporary France are the fruit of Cardijn's initiative and ideas in Belgium, passing through French minds and applied, more successfully than in any other country, to the dechristianised proletariat masses of France.

When Cardijn gave his *Ite, Missa Est* conference in Rheims, in 1933, he had no more sympathetic listener in his audience than Mgr. Suhard, Archbishop of Rheims and future Cardinal Archbishop of Paris, who himself had established the Y.C.W. in his diocese. Replying to Cardijn on this important occasion, Mgr. Suhard said:

> We only need to hear Canon Cardijn speak in order to be won over to his cause. Those who have been in touch with the Y.C.W., if they are fair-minded persons, are bound to be impressed by what they have seen and observed. This sympathy which they cannot help feeling is to be explained by the fact that from the J.O.C. springs the realisation of basic truths. This seems to be its special mark: it intends to see realised a conviction about the three following points: (1) It is within the actuality of professional life itself that Christian renewal must take place. (2) This renewal must, in the first instance, be an individual renewal of the worker himself, since a man cannot give what he does not himself possess. (3) The worker will never be fully Christian unless he is also an apostle. If we could persuade all Catholics of this truth, and not workers only; if we could form them into this way of seeing things and inspire in them the will to be missionary Catholics, what a tremendous leap forward we would take. Besides, this method is historically the Church's method, as well as being founded on individual psychology, for how can one fully live a Christian life if one is not concerned to live it outwardly, to make it loved and understood around one, to infuse it within the whole of our society?[1]

[1] *Ite, Missa Est*, pp. 22-4.

And Mgr. Suhard expounded the four needs of the worker-missionaries: an ideal which the leaders must teach; a discipline among Jocists, among their leaders and among their priests; a doctrine, 'not an ideology, nor mere religious sentiment; that is not enough; but a doctrine adapted to the worker's life and which teaches the worker to live his job in a Christian way'; and the strength to live the ideal, 'a strength to be found first in the priest who must be an apostle giving to the laity the example, the "form", of the apostolate by making use of the facts which the worker brings to him, by enlarging on them, and by making them fruitful with the knowledge he possesses of doctrine in general'.[1]

It cannot be doubted that the foundation and method of the Y.C.W., together with the personality of Cardijn, and its introduction into France played an important part in forming the bold mind and new apostolic plans of the great Cardinal, but the work of renewing, through fresh approaches, the Catholic life of a largely paganised France was more directly brought to Cardinal Suhard's attention along another road which was more of a by-product of Cardijn and the Y.C.W.

Among the chaplains of the French Y.C.W. was a strange, untidy priest, his mind full of new notions and half-digested ideas, destined to become famous. His name was Godin. Like Cardijn, he was born of the people. Restless and frustrated in his little country parish, he sought exciting and profitable apostolic work in the real contemporary world and he found it in the world where the Y.C.W. was at work. The young workers adored this 'walking muddle' with his bold mind, his deep humility, his strong, simple spirituality.

Godin's mind, stimulated and excited by the Cardijn vision and method, did not, however, share the patience,

[1] Ibid.

orderliness and methodical toughness of the Founder of the
Y.C.W. nor was he interested in economics and social
problems as such. His real interest was in the religious
problems of the working people. A fresh approach—
actually in germ in the Y.C.W. ideology—came to him
after talking to a foreign missionary who explained the
foreign missionary technique of building up Christian
communities within pagan countries. That was how he
came to be struck by the idea that contemporary France,
with its great masses of dechristianised peoples, was, in
its own way, just as much a missionary country as the
distant parts of the globe. The period was the Second
World War when, under enemy occupation, life was fluid
and uncertain. The Y.C.W. itself could not carry on its
normal public activities, and Godin's own attempts to rally
it met with opposition from the Germans. The Y.C.W.
had, in fact, to go into hiding; many of its members were
deported or joined the Maquis, its chaplain was arrested.
It could only continue its work within the parishes, thus
suffering to some extent from traditional parish weakness in facing the problems of evangelising the *milieu*
of the workers and the paganised even within the parish
boundaries.

Godin, moreover, dreamt of quicker results than the
Cardijn method allowed, and even envisaged the Y.C.W.
confining itself to social problems, while he dealt with the
religious ones. In particular, the Y.C.W. had not, he
thought, successfully met the problem created by the age
limits within which it worked. He concluded that, despite
the Y.C.W., 'The masses escape us; we are not reaching
them.' And in so far as they were reached, they were
gradually lost as the young workers married and became
preoccupied with the new problems of full manhood and
womanhood.

Whether Godin was right or wrong about this, it was

certainly his association with the Y.C.W. and his love of it which had launched him into the undertaking, together with another Y.C.W. chaplain, the Abbé Daniel, of a practical inquiry into the real facts of Christianity in France, the *Rapport sur la conquête chrétienne des milieux prolétariens* which became famous under the popular title: *La France pays de mission?*

In this book was demonstrated the now accepted fact that today a Christian country can be divided into two separate 'nations', however mixed together locally, a 'nation' where Christian values are accepted and a 'nation' which lives by pagan or secularised values. Cardijn had, in effect, said exactly the same, though the stronger Christian tradition of his own country had helped him to look for the 'pagan' nation more exclusively within the workers, of whom he saw himself as a member. To Cardijn's youth apostolate combined with social reform, in the application of Christian principles for the workers, corresponded Godin's foreign missionary conception of a new apostolic technique. Freed from traditional Catholic and French parochial ways, the pattern of foreign missionary work within an indigenous apostolate could be adapted to serve the dechristianised masses. In fact, of course, the dechristianised nation in France was virtually the working class, and the distinction between Cardijn's method in practice and Godin's was not so very great. With Cardijn, the worker-apostles naturally used a technique suitable to their fellow-workers, and would surely use it more easily and naturally than Godin's few selected priests could possibly do. Nor, of course, could Cardijn accept any division between the spiritual and the social approach.

But Godin's book created a tremendous stir and it made a deep impression on Cardinal Suhard. Moved to action, the Cardinal gathered together in the Mission de Paris a number of priests who would undertake to carry out Godin's plan of trying with new methods, and extra-parochially, to bring back the faith to the paganised nation. The enterprise suffered from the first, however, from the lack of precision and practicality in Godin's mind. They had been told what needed to be done, but were left with very little idea of how it was to be done. The first priests belonging to this special mission were nearly all ex-Y.C.W. chaplains.

From a quite different source, but running parallel with Godin's plan, there then arose the priest-worker conception. This derived from the accident that chaplains had secretly been appointed to help French workers deported to Germany for forced labour. In carrying out this difficult and dangerous mission, they discovered remarkable new apostolic and priestly opportunities deriving from the simple fact that the outward distinction between priest and flock had disappeared. From the idea of perpetuating this experience in places where the soutane and traditional clerical values and ways formed in themselves a solid wall between priests and people, arose the controverted priest-worker movement.

Though we have run far ahead in time through following out these well-known apostolic developments in France, they greatly help in forming a picture of the spiritual and apostolic potentiality of Cardijn's work as it existed in the middle twenties. It is clear that what might be called the awakening of the Church in France to the new situations, new conditions and new opportunities of the apostolate—an awakening generally acknowledged to be the inspiration of much liturgical change and reform in the Church today— has owed a great deal to what Cardijn had accomplished by 1927. Once the essence of the Cardijn teaching that the hope of the Church and therefore the hope of the de-christianised world lay in bracketing 'Christian' with 'Christian missionary or apostle' was understood, of like working with like, the full implications of the truth were bound to express themselves in all sorts of ways. For the ordinary Christian to be an apostle involved a training, a formation, a trust, a zeal, a spiritual outlook in sharp contrast with the pastoral conception which had permeated the Church, especially in the defensive centuries of the post-Reformation period when defence of the Church and protection of the faithful from an anti-Catholic environment were felt to be the first necessities.

That this attack—in the form of going out to live, spread and preach Christianity in a world enslaved by its own failure to understand human nature—was also by far the best form of defence, was the lesson which Cardijn could not have taught from the pulpit or by his writing, but only by the practical experiment he had made with the least considered, the least hopeful, stratum of society: the young workers who were the most obvious victims of the modern secularist set-up.

Impatient of the slow and age-limited progress of the Y.C.W. yet owing much to the lessons it was teaching, Godin was actually taking a backward step when he ceased to concentrate on the lay apostolate in a frustrated lay world living a life outside Christian values, and sought to establish a new type of missionary priest, thus easing the way for the priest-worker. He found only a few volunteers, who were puzzled by the task assigned to them, while the priest-worker, inevitably divided in his allegiance to his fellow-priests or his worker comrades, could hardly avoid running into difficulties. It is indeed desirable, today as much as yesterday, that every priest should be a missionary, truly understanding and sharing the lives of his people; but the priest as priest could never share the life of the worker, the farmer, the sailor, the student, as the lay apostle could. It was these, in their potentially unlimited numbers, who had to be formed by truly missionary and understanding priests to carry Christ within their own *milieu.*

H

However slow and difficult the work, given human nature both in the conservatism of ecclesiastical ways and in the weakness of the average Christian layman and woman, the secret so obviously lay in the Cardijn prescription that it simply had to win the day and thus profoundly affect the Church's whole apostolate. It must win, even if any one experiment like the Y.C.W. were to fail to make headway or become outdated. That, in fact, it proved strong enough and flexible enough to make far more progress than Cardijn, as he now confesses, ever thought possible—that it became the model for other lay apostolates, will now be seen.

7

WORLD FAME
(1927–1931)

THERE is a sense in which it can be said that the Cardijn
Story has already been told, for one of the things that most
vividly strikes the outsider about Cardijn's life and about
his movement is the way in which their future is contained
in their past. This is the note of a genuinely organic and
vital movement. The oak is contained in the acorn, the
man in the embryo, and if we could see deeply enough into
these, we could foretell the lines of their future development,
subject though these are, in the vegetable and animal, to
their future environment and, in man, to the way he will
choose his human destiny. But in man-made social plans,
future development even of the germinal idea is subject to
constant alterations even to the original conception, as vital
new experiences are met with; while most social developments can hardly be said to have had a germinal idea at
all, but to grow as the result of theories carefully worked out
a priori by various people—theories which, if something constructive is to emerge, mingle together through processes
of trial and error. Not the least remarkable characteristic
of Cardijn's Jocism is its logical predetermined growth,
development and adaptation to environment from Cardijn's
vitally concrete will to apply the Christ-in-the-Church
apostolic mission to that section of society whose spiritual
and human needs had been most consistently disregarded.
Translate that aim into practical terms which take into
account the Gospels, the authority and organisation of the

Church and the working-class *milieu* of the time, but refusing to take into account the mere conservatisms, the conventions, the fears, the 'what is done' mentality, which have overlaid clerical and secular society, and you have the future of Jocism. In only one respect was the basic conception arbitrarily limited through the inevitable limitations of any one man's experience and keenest interest, namely in its being a movement for youth, and specifically worker youth. But in principle it is universally applicable to the essential Christianising task within a world where Christians as a whole have lost the dynamic missionary meaning of Christ's revelation and where non-Christians have drited into materialism, secularism, and paganism—the best name for which is 'post-Christianity'.

When we begin fully to understand this, we shall also understand the providential inevitableness of the extraordinary way in which a little unknown curate in 1925 found only in the Pope himself the embrace and the welcome which carried his work forward in the face of criticisms and condemnations. It was he who had to tell the Pope of the true conditions of the workers and of the failure of Catholics to do much about them

No wonder that once the movement had been officially established it was to Rome that Cardijn always looked, and it was to Rome that Cardijn repaired every year. 'How is the work going?' Pius XI would ask him. 'Do people now believe in the J.O.C.?' And Cardijn had to confess then, as he has to confess today: 'Holy Father, there are still some who do not believe.' And then, in 1927, the Pope answered: 'Come with your leaders to Rome. The Pope will show the world and he will show to all priests what he thinks of the workers and what he thinks of your movement.'

It took two years to prepare and organise the response to that Papal invitation.

For Cardijn, this pilgrimage across Europe to Rome was

not only a question of bringing as many of the Belgian Jocists as possible to see and hear his friend, Pius XI, the Vicar of Christ; it was also a symbol of the emancipation of the young workers whose longest journeys hitherto had been a few kilometres in the Belgian plain to this or that place of spiritual or cultural interest, to the sea perhaps or some pleasant country spot.

The plan was to take no fewer than 1,500 of these young men across Europe into Switzerland and thence through Italy to Rome for a full week's holiday as well as pilgrimage. The broadening of horizons involved in this actual journey to places known to them only through pictures or the cinema screen was a symbol of all that he had wanted for a class of men condemned by society and their circumstances of life to exist cut off from their heritage as Christians and as men. It had not always been so. In the so-called Dark Ages, no class division, no enslavement to long hours of factory work, prevented the pilgrims of Christendom from long journey-ings on foot to Rome, to Compostella and other great shrines, and to us it is still extraordinary to read of this constant traffic within Europe, in which rich and poor took part. Despite the fact that trains now enabled such journeys to be made in a few hours, instead of weeks and months, the mass of the workers could neither afford the time nor the money for experiences that could enhance their personalities and strengthen their sense of Christian heritage. In making possible this great journey, Cardijn, as always, was carrying out the purpose of his movement on its temporal as well as spiritual side.

At last the day had come—mid-September 1929. The 1,500 young men (many of them heavily encumbered with their working clothes, their tools and samples of their work, for it was as workers offering their work that they would greet the Holy Father) were carried in three trains south through Luxemburg to Basle, from Basle to the Lake of

Lucerne, which they reached on the Monday morning in time to fill two churches for the hearing of Mass. For the travellers, whose eyes, as long as they could remember, had been accustomed to the shadows, grime and shapelessness of the industrial districts of Belgium, the glistening waters of the famous lake, cupped within the shadows and sunshine reflected from the rocky slopes of the mountains, must have seemed like some incomprehensible mirage, as they were carried over it in the little steamers down the lake of the Four Cantons to Fluelen. One can imagine the exaltation in the heart of the forty-year-old priest who had suffered so much and fought so hard to make such a workers' playtime possible. As he watched them all around him, he could think of what it meant to them, singing in their hearts with the psalmist: 'I lift up my heart to the hills, to find deliverance; from the Lord deliverance comes to me, the Lord who made heaven and earth.'

Entraining once more at Fluelen, the now delivered masses continued southwards all night through the St. Gothard by the Lake of Como to reach Milan where in the cathedral they knelt by the tomb of St. Charles Borromeo.

For Cardijn himself, next to Rome must have come Assisi, for in the spirit of St. Francis—a Franciscan missionary zeal for the twentieth century—he had found so much of his own inspiration. Through Assisi and all it symbolised of the love of Christ he led them. Then at last, on the Wednesday evening, the 1,500 shared the sight so ardently longed for by Christians throughout the centuries: the myriad lights against the shadowy evening outline of the Eternal City with its dome of Peter. To the rhythm of the wheels of the trains as they hammered onwards, the pilgrims sang the canticle of the Magnificat, 'he has put down the mighty from their seat, and exalted the lowly; he has filled the hungry with good things, and sent the rich away empty-handed'. How true these young people must have felt those words to be, as they thought of the spiritual riches and inspiration which were now awaiting them, representatives of millions who had been deprived of the enjoyment of their human right.

All had been arranged with the organising skill that the movement had made its own from the start. Each pilgrim knew where he was to sleep and how to get there. These self-disciplined bands, having sung their Jocist song, left the station within a few minutes of arrival, much to the astonishment of the Fascist-led people of Rome who had despaired of self-discipline.

Next morning, the 1,500 were together again, walking in two long columns, their flags flying, within the colonnade of St. Peter's. The first great moment for Cardijn had come. His young workers were at last to enter St. Peter's to hear Mass celebrated by their own Cardinal Van Roey (who had insisted on being with them himself) and to visit the tomb of the Apostles.

Then came the pilgrimage to the great basilicas, and in the Lateran Palace they gathered to hear Tonnet speak by the statue of the metal-worker with his tools, erected there to commemorate Leo XIII and his 1891 *Rerum Novarum* Encyclical on the Condition of the Workers. On the pedestal are inscribed the words: *Patri et Vindici Opifices:* the Workers to their Father and Vindicator.

The visit to the Colosseum afforded Cardijn another great text from which to preach to his disciples, for were not Peter and Paul and many of the early Christian martyrs themselves workers whose faith in Christ gave them the strength to challenge, by love and the friendship which links man with man in Christ, the Roman slave-state and ultimately to destroy it?

Next day, the workers penetrated into the catacombs to find confirmation of what Cardijn had brought home to them in the Colosseum. Surrounded by the tombs of the martyrs with all the evidence they furnish of the half-light in which early Christianity lived, just as a half-light had been needed for the development in the twentieth century of the movement to bring Christ back to the secularised worker-masses, they heard Mass all together in the underground chapel of St. Domitilla.

Strengthened by these days of practical formation, in which not intellect alone but the heart, the will and all the senses had been moved as never before—a miraculous heightening and concentration of the method dear to Cardijn's whole genius—the 1,500, on the Saturday afternoon, were ready for the climax: the audience with Pope Pius XI.

Once more, they gathered together in their long columns in the square of St. Peter's, but this time they were dressed in the clothes of their trades. Miners were there with their helmets and their lamps; metal-workers with their leather aprons and their tools; railway workers in their uniform blue; painters in their white blouses; carpenters with their planes; and dozens of other trades were represented. Rome had never seen such a sight. The Italians gaped and chattered excitedly around them. Strict rules of etiquette lay down the proper formal clothes in which the Pope of Rome must be visited. Cardijn himself had broken the ice four years before with his old soutane; his followers today carried the habits and ensigns of their labouring lives with an honest pride of children visiting their father, not courtiers visiting a monarch. As children, too, they were to offer their father the best of presents—the presents they had worked to produce: the finest pieces of cloth they had woven; the jewellery they had lovingly shaped; the books they had bound and incised with the Papal arms; even the produce of the land which they had tilled.

This unprecedented sight had filled the great piazza, and through the crowds the Jocist columns entered the Vatican by the bronze doors as the Swiss Guards saluted. Up the great staircase and through the halls and apartments of a royal residence, the tread of the marching workers resounded on the marble floors. It was not the first time the workers had marched into royal palaces; but hitherto they had been workers moved by fury and hatred, and intent on creating a new order by destruction. Never had they succeeded in their aims. Now for the first time workers were invading a royal palace with love and hope in their hearts, visiting a prince to pay him homage, to acclaim him as their leader, to inaugurate a new age and a revolution by love and trust. For that prince was the vicar of Him in whom these young workers had resolved to place their one hope.

Now they were lined up awaiting the Pope. Their leader was ready to accompany the Holy Father along the Jocist columns and introduce the worker-pilgrims. When the white figure appeared he was greeted with acclamation and, accompanied by Cardijn, the Pope moved slowly along the lines of those first representatives of the hundreds of thousands—workers, soldiers, students, men and women of every class and condition—who in the years to come would find Pius XI and his successor, Pius XII, waiting to hear, encourage and bless them. The precedent had been dramatically established by these bands of workers in their working-clothes.

After the Pope had spoken to each pilgrim and offered his ring to be kissed, the young workers were guided towards the great hall of beatifications behind the balcony whence the Pope blesses the crowds in the piazza. At length the 1,500 were massed in the hall, and Pius XI moved to his throne, to the sound of cheering. Once more a precedent was broken when Tonnet addressed the Pope on behalf of the pilgrimage, for protocol ruled that only ambassadors could speak to the Pope without first being spoken to.

Pius XI greeted his visitors with unusual emotion and

spoke to them in the colloquial and familiar language which a father uses in talking to his own favourite children. He had already in June spoken of missionary movements in which the laity carried Christian values into the special entourage of their work and interests—movements of which the Y.C.W. was the pioneer—as 'the apple of his eye'; and now that the Jocists were with him he said to them: 'It is you who are the Church within your factories and within the *milieu* of your work. It falls to you to win over working youth.' And he gave the fullest possible authentication of Cardijn's work with the words: 'We have defined Catholic Action, and this definition has been perfectly interpreted by the Y.C.W. and in its publications which we know well.' Such work, he said, was true missionary work, and just as there are foreign missions in countries where Christianity has not been preached so there are missionaries of the interior who carry out the Christian apostolate where it is needed at home. To missionaries he gave as patron St. Teresa of Lisieux, a saint who—in acquiring a universal popularity in modern times because her sanctity was built on a humble but perfect fidelity in little things—suited well the Christian zeal of hidden workers whose individual successes would never be heard of.

The great journey and pilgrimage were over, and Cardijn and the 1,500 Jocists, representatives of so many more left behind, could return home meditating, as Cardijn was meditating, that 'no king, no emperor, was ever received by the common Father of the faithful as they had been received'. The return journey was through the Mt. Cenis and France, after a halt in Turin where the pilgrims prayed by the tomb of Don Bosco, another pioneer of the apostolate of the workers. The common workers' round awaited them at home, but in future it would be done with a new and wider vision, a new and deeper hope.

The 1929 pilgrimage to Rome inevitably made a

tremendous impression in the Catholic world. This romantic band of lay worker-apostles had not only come into contact with many people in Italy itself and impinged on the attention of the influential in Rome, but the reports of all that had happened had been read by Catholics and others all over the world. For the first time it was widely realised in the Church that something new and fresh had emerged, fully contemporary with the times. Communism and socialism were in the ascendant, profiting from the visible failure of the democratic tradition to give to the ordinary man economic opportunity and security in a world that was growing yearly more unsettled and unsure of itself. Unemployment was increasing and as the circle of unemployment widened so were great sections of the masses being denied the basic means of even decent human existence. In Europe, more and more thinking and feeling people, despairing of their liberal heritage, were turning politically and culturally 'leftward' under the illusion that a solution could be found in the totalitarian control of nations for the benefit of the working masses. Nor were those who thought this way made at all unhappy by the prospect of an ever more materialistic and anti-religious organisation of society under Marxist leadership. Religion was associated with the ruling and bourgeois classes which had manifestly failed to create an equitable and progressive social order. The ideal of freedom for its own sake and for the individual as such was rapidly giving way to the ideal of opportunity for the dispossessed at the expense of the possessing, and the word freedom was reinterpreted to signify the emancipation of the masses by any means, however unfree. Democracy was rapidly acquiring a new meaning, all the more easily accepted because it was set against the solution of the 'right wing', the rich, the bourgeois, the establishment who saw in the open Fascist rejection of democracy and parliamentarianism the real hope of the future. In

Germany the Nazi movement was making ominous headway, just when in apparently prosperous America the great
financial collapse left to Europe the legacy of slump and
unprecedented unemployment.

In a world shaken by these contending forces, the
emergence of Cardijn's Jocist movement could in itself be
no more than a tiny, unfelt pin-prick. But it curiously bore
the mark of the times. Externally, its rallies, its manifestations, its flags, its songs corresponded with the sense of
public challenge which was making itself felt everywhere,
both on the political Left and on the Right. In its expression of the rights of the workers, of the common people,
once again it was in harmony with the claims of the rival
camps. But, against the rapidly discredited parliamentarianism and democracy, even when under Christian
leadership, it pointed to the crying need, namely the need
for the prior formation of workers so that they might be
capable of envisaging a positive and truly free ideal on the
basis of which a healthy social democracy must rest.

Thus the end of the 1920s and the early 1930s was a time
which in one sense greatly favoured the expansion and influence of the Jocist movement among some Catholics and
yet, in another, provoked criticism and misunderstanding.
At last, there was something Christian on the right lines,
yet this something, many felt, might prove highly dangerous
in its defiant protective interest in that working class which
was the cause of all the trouble. Fear is a stronger emotion
than hope, so that while the Y.C.W. could come out more
bravely than ever in its apostolic and social colours under
the Pope's protection, it became more suspect than ever to
many a *bien-pensant*.

External manifestation followed external manifestation,
whether in rallies and congresses in Belgium, or in pilgrimages that caught the international eye. Cardijn himself, after the 1929 Rome pilgrimage, was at last formally

raised above his ecclesiastical status of 'a little curate' and made an honorary canon. Two years later, the celebration of the twenty-fifth anniversary of his ordination as a priest, his Silver Jubilee, was marked by another great pilgrimage to Rome and the Holy Father, this time with the J.O.C.F., the girls and young women of his movement, which, though completely divided as to the sexes, was one single movement. On this pilgrimage, his memory must have carried him back very vividly to the early days in Laeken where he found the girl apprentices and workers of the parish the seed of so much that was to come. The growing French J.O.C. was not to be behindhand in demonstrations of strength and in seeking the Pope's counsel and blessing. For this, the founder, Canon Cardijn, must be with them.

But Cardijn's own choice of Jocist celebration to mark his jubilee takes us back to the earliest days and the earliest devotion of his life, the one that had been inspired by the church of Hal with its miraculous statue of the Virgin Mary. He invited as many of his followers as could to join him on a pilgrimage of thanksgiving to Lourdes. In gratitude to him and to the Blessed Virgin, no fewer than 5,000 accompanied him. The numbers were too great to fit into the basilica so, at an altar set up outside, Canon Cardijn sang his Jubilee High Mass, at which the Bishop of Lourdes, Mgr. (later Cardinal) Gerlier, preached. To the priest the occasion was so moving that in attempting to express his thanks to the great gathering around him he broke down. He could not find the words wherewith to express those twenty-five years of struggle, suffering and misunderstanding which, providentially and with the help of our Lady, had come to bear a visible fruit far beyond his own hopes. To our Lady he vowed his lifelong devotion to the first of his aims, even as a boy: to save the working class.

But for Cardijn in 1931 something else took place which, in its implications, must have proved for him a consolation

no less deep than his priestly jubilee—indeed, it was the
real crown to his life's work so far.

When he was nine years old, he heard of Leo XIII's
Workers' Charter, that official Papal instruction which was
to guide his own steps. But Cardijn could not follow without also moving forward in the light of the evidence and the
action which the evidence demanded. Now his friend,
Pius XI, gave to the world the follow-up to *Rerum Novarum*
forty years after, *Quadragesimo Anno*, and within it was
formally enshrined that form of Catholic Action and even
that very movement, almost in so many words, which
Cardijn had pioneered.

> Nowadays, as more than once in the history of the Church
> [the Pope wrote], we are confronted with a world which in
> large measure has almost fallen back into paganism. In order
> to bring back to Christ those whole classes of men who have
> denied him, we must gather and train from amidst their very
> ranks auxiliary soldiers of the Church, men who know their
> mentality and their aspirations, and who with kindly fraternal
> charity will be able to win their hearts. Undoubtedly the first
> and immediate apostles of the working men must themselves
> be working men, while the apostles of the industrial and com-
> mercial world should themselves be employers and merchants.

'The apostles of the working men must themselves be working men', how often Cardijn, in one way or another, had
said that. It had been the essence of his movement. But
Pius XI referred almost by name to the Y.C.W. when he
wrote: 'To the great joy of our heart, we discern amongst
them dense masses of young workers, who listen readily to
the call of divine grace and strive with splendid zeal to win
their fellows to Christ.' And finally, Pius XI accepted the
Y.C.W. tactic in distinguishing between Catholic Action
and the practical work of social reform within industrial
relations. The latter is the concern of those who have been
formed through Catholic Action: 'We look for this [social

reform], not to Catholic Action . . . but to our sons, whom
Catholic Action imbues with these principles and trains for
the apostolate.' This vitally interconnected, yet in itself
dual, role corresponds accurately to Michael Fogarty's
classification of the Y.C.W. movement:

> Thus the Young Christian Workers would ordinarily be
> classified as an organisation of Catholic Action, indeed one of
> the most important of them. Yet this is also certainly an
> organisation in which laymen have a very high degree of
> responsibility, and which aims at and achieves important
> political, economic and social ends. For certain purposes it is
> convenient to think of it rather as a branch of Christian
> Democracy.[1]

These years which made Jocism a new name and a new
force within the Church—though the observer is bound to
express surprise at the limited general Catholic interest in
that name and force in view of the uniquely high sponsor-
ship which it was given—imposed rapidly increasing
responsibilities on the Brussels secretariat.

In 1928 the *mansardes* of the rue Plétinckx—so dear to
Cardijn, the three musketeers and the other early leaders—
with its catacomb-like memories of the early struggles and
hopes, and the now almost legendary stories of its beginnings, had to be given up in favour of a handsome, large and
rather surprisingly bourgeois house in the rue des Palais,
so well-known today to the many people who want to see
the veteran Mgr. Cardijn himself, for it is now his residence
as Chaplain-General of the world movement. This house
of many floors with its steep staircase that alarms the tired
visitor but has no terrors for its seventy-year-old owner, who
must have tripped up and down it thousands of times, did
not long remain Y.C.W. headquarters, so rapidly was progress now being made. By 1934, the greatest external

[1] Op. cit., pp. 5, 6.

change in the movement was made. The Y.C.W. suddenly impinged on the city of Brussels and, more indirectly, on the world as an imposing mass of masonry dominating the southern end of the wide Boulevard Poincaré, near the South Station, the gateway of Belgium to France and the great seaways which were carrying the message of Jocism across the world.

This dramatic scene-change in the Jocist story did not, unfortunately, betoken a comparable increase in its material resources. As we have seen, Cardijn's mixture of *mystique* and hard-headed realism, expressed so well in his sense of the importance of each member's subscription as a symbol of responsibility and dedication, made him always insist on the movement solidly paying its way with the money in hand. Alas, the amount of money in hand did not remotely permit of such sudden transformations. Yet the increase in work made a move from the rue des Palais essential. What was to be done? Cardijn had been invited by the Cardinal Archbishop of Lisbon to go to Portugal and give lectures there on Catholic Action. While in that country, he made the pilgrimage to Fatima and in that remote spot, in the spirit of the child in Hal, he prayed that the Blessed Virgin should help the movement to find a solution for its material problems.

On his return to Brussels he was informed that a gigantic new building in the Boulevard Poincaré, intended to be a great hosiery factory, was for sale. His informant advised him to see the owner and to ask him to allow the building to be used as the headquarters of the J.O.C. Cardijn went to see the owner, who was not even a practising Catholic, and, naturally enough, he was not well received. However, the owner referred him to his agent on a normal business footing to see whether a normal business deal could be arranged. Naturally, it could not be, and the agent was no more welcoming than the owner. Then something happened, the exact nature of which it seems today impossible to trace. A third party mysteriously intervened, and the great building was handed over to Cardijn as a gift to the J.O.C. But even this astonishing answer to Cardijn's prayer meant only the winning of half the battle. A building constructed as a hosiery factory would not be internally of much use as the headquarters of a movement responsible for all the ramifications of organisation, record-keeping, propaganda and dozens of technical office jobs. An immense sum was needed to make the required conversion. 'What trials our Lady sends us!' Cardijn exclaimed—rather ungratefully in the circumstances, it seems. And nothing spectacular happened this time. But the money needed came in, and the work could be undertaken.

In fact, the building was far larger than was strictly needed for the business in hand, but as the *Centrale Jociste* it providentially served purposes of the utmost advantage to the movement as a whole. It became, and has remained, a real heart, a real centre, of the world movement. The vast spaces could be used for a worthy chapel, a great lecture or conference room, a library, canteens, dining and recreation rooms attractive to members, guests and passers-by. Magnificently run, in the Cardijn spirit of efficiency, it must be unique, at any rate in the old world, as the headquarters of a Catholic Action movement which, at the time, was still only emerging. And, not least important, from its roof a great forty-foot statue of a young worker, carrying a shield with the letters K.A.J.O.C. (Flemish-Walloon combination of the Y.C.W. initials), proclaimed to the capital the challenge of Canon Cardijn's Young Catholic Workers in those days of unemployment, depression, ideological conflict and fears of the catastrophe of a second war.

In considering in these pages the work of the inspirer and founder of the movement, there is, of course, the danger of giving a false impression of the work as a whole

I

at this stage of its development. Moreover, it is a danger which would be actually injurious to Cardijn's own genius and reputation, for it was the unique quality of Cardijn's Y.C.W. at the time that within it, as a clerico-lay movement, the fullest autonomy and responsibility was given to its lay members. In its organisation, building-up and especially on the social plane, Cardijn's Y.C.W. was a hundred per cent. lay movement. Readers of Marguerite Fièvez's life of Fernand Tonnet are given a just picture of the Y.C.W. development in Belgium as Tonnet's movement, even more than Cardijn's. And it was Cardijn himself who described Tonnet as the movement's head, Garcet as its heart and Meert as its hands. The fact that this was so, constitutes the greatest compliment to Cardijn and brings out his uniqueness as a priest-founder of a Catholic organisation. He was, as someone said, the movement's *flamme*, a word that loses much of its sense of an inspiring, heartening, almost passion-giving force when translated into English as flame. Marguerite Fièvez has herself expressed what it meant:

> In them and through them [Tonnet, Garcet, Meert] was realised the idea which, for twenty-five years, lay at the heart of Cardijn's priestly life. Now he could see all around him the kind of worker-apostles of which he had dreamt. In fact, he seemed to be already entrusting to them his own destiny: it was they who incarnated the new Workers' Youth. It was he who did the thinking. It was he who contributed the richness of his creative genius, who unfolded the new aspects of the problem to be solved, who launched the young people on the slipway. Above all, his was the inspiration which gave to their individual and collective activities a supernatural dynamism that astounded those with whom they came into contact. Always he would be, for the three founder-members, the young curate of Laeken and of the Central Study-Circle. Their faith in the way he had led them would always remain unshaken. Many chaplains from abroad were

struck in the international meetings of 1931 by this: 'Cardijn sees it this way' Tonnet would say, and with those words, would close the discussion.[1]

Autocrat-democrat, paternalist with the fullest confidence in the judgment and powers of his own children, this natural and vital balance, so rarely acquired, so hard to maintain, was behind the whole movement, and it was the very confidence which Cardijn could inspire through his own assurance and gift of leadership which, uniquely, enabled the movement to be the responsible work of its young lay members, not of its inspirer and guide.

Tonnet himself, now forty years of age, and from the beginning completely devoted to the cause of the working class in its most personal and practical aspects, had felt it necessary to resign from the Presidency and carry on his mission outside the scope of the Y.C.W. The resignation of the 'first Jocist', as Fernand Tonnet was called, was a sad occasion for the pioneers, marking in yet another way the ending of the first phase of the movement, the foundation and Belgian phase, even though with France and other countries, the international phase, as we shall see, was rapidly opening out. In particular it was sad for Cardijn who said: 'For me, Fernand has been like a blessing and a grace in my priestly life.' It was he who providentially had been the perfect lay complement to the priest-founder, thus establishing from the start the necessary balance within the movement if it was not either to fall back into the normal essentially clerical Catholic movement or be tempted to break away from Cardijn's special apostolic ideal and become, in effect, another political and social form of trade-unionism, however Christian.

Tonnet himself, shortly after leaving, found himself in opposition to his old friends in that he wanted to start a special trade-union section for the younger workers within

[1] *Fernand Tonnet*, pp. 195–6.

the Confederation of Christian Trade Unions in Belgium. The Y.C.W. had to argue that trade-union formation for young Christian workers could best be promoted by the Y.C.W., since it was in a position to provide a full and integrated formation of those who would have to carry on later in the Christian Trade Unions. And as a result of the arguments and discussions on this point the definite affiliation of the Young Christian Workers with the Confederation of Christian Trade Unions within the National Christian Labour Movement was permanently established. It was in the logic of things that this affiliation, which might have come much earlier, should have been made—and made, oddly enough, as an unexpected result of Tonnet's resignation and his desire to carry into new fields what he had learned within the Y.C.W. through Cardijn.

8

MODEL FOR THE WORLD
(1935)

THE following words, put into the mouth of his Y.C.W. hero by Maxence van der Meersch, well represent the early Cardijn fighting his never-ending battle to break down the barriers, the wall, between the Church and the workers of the twentieth century.

All my life long I shall see the strange figure of this little priest, abruptly jumping to his feet on the platform, coming, going, shouting, throwing himself about, waving his arms, making sudden gestures with his hands. He seemed so thin, so spare, so austere, as he threw out unfinished phrases, blowing, panting, gesticulating, almost comic in his violence. At first some girls near us were inclined to smile, but gradually his very enthusiasm, his fire, his sincerity, his indignation, his eagerness, his tenderness, and his pity had the effect of moving the whole place, stirring the whole crowd to its depths, making it gasp, thrill, grow excited and weep, caught at its very heart by the sight of this man giving himself absolutely, to the depths of his soul, nay, almost to blood, for the cause of the unfortunate and the oppressed for whom his Master had died. In this priest's tears, his passion, his despair, his dreams, his immense love for the wretched, the great High Priest himself was incarnate; in him we were beholding Christ; through his voice unmistakably Christ once again was declaring to men their duty.[1]

This was the technique of the platform-speaker, of the

[1] *Fishers of Men*, pp. 41–2.

hustings, in which he had trained himself from his earliest student days. What a politician he would have made, with this power to translate through his whole being and dramatically to pour into the minds and feelings of his hearers all that he himself knew, willed and felt.

But no politician could have used comparable oratorical gifts to so fruitful a purpose as the transformation of the moral and human outlook of the simple working men and women tempted to find in hatred, violence and totalitarian political ideologies the only answers to the wrongs they suffered.

This emotional platform oratory was by no means Cardijn's only form of public expression, and those who know him best will say that he was far greater as Cardijn, priest and teacher, before the smaller gatherings and study conferences of his followers, especially with the leaders and the chaplains. On such occasions, the fiery, self-giving orator returned to the schoolroom at Wavre and, with a logical precision brought down to earth by practical example from a rich experience, he would teach more and more implications and applications of the veritable new world of apostolic and social ideas and values that were contained in those simple propositions that were the kernel of his message to Church and world. In typed summaries of the main heads of such lectures, one finds again and again in the strong, clear, sloping handwriting of those days notes like: 'Deepen these statements.'—'Back these truths by facts.'—'Answer every question personally.'—'The case of a leader . . .'—'The case of a young worker . . .', each with practical details as to how success was achieved, bad company avoided, and the like.

In this personal teaching, his task was never to end, for Cardijn's lifelong faith in youth and its possibilities in the formation of lives, one's own and that of others, means that his work has had to be renewed again and again. Just as in a school, class after class comes before the master as the years follow one another, so Cardijn has had to form class after class of leaders, and form them so well that they could form others. The process quickly stales most men, but Cardijn seemed able continuously to deepen and widen the applications of his basic principles. Again and again, he says basically the same thing, yet always differently, always more widely applied to the conditions of this world and the times.

Lastly, there was Cardijn, the orator and preacher of the great occasion, when princes of the Church, leading statesmen and experts were there to hear him. Though French was not truly his native language, he had a mastery of it which seems almost incompatible with his rough upbringing and lack of academic formation. And what in others might have been a weakness, he could use to good purpose in that even on these occasions he remained simple and concrete.

These speaking gifts were now to be tested to their utmost, for the year 1935 was the tenth of the movement— a chance not to be missed by an organisation that was so well aware of the importance of the best showmanship. And it surely had a right to make itself felt and seen before the world of now rapidly mounting ideological conflict, for in those ten years it had come of age in Belgium and in France and its first penetration had been made into a number of other countries.

A year of preparation had gone into the making of this jubilee celebration of Sunday, 25 August 1935, to be followed by four days of the first international Study Conference, and Cardijn had insisted that every penny of expense should be borne by the movement itself, the unemployed themselves not hesitating to make their contribution. Now it was no longer a question of the few thousands of the earlier years but of figures mounting up to near 100,000.

No church could remotely hope to house the religious ceremony, and it was in the royal park of Laeken, under the distant windows of the royal palace, that the Cardinal Archbishop of Malines would sing pontifical High Mass in the presence of Cardinal Verdier of Paris and the Cardinal Patriarch of Lisbon, the Belgian Episcopate, Bishop Myers from London, Van Zeeland the Belgian Prime Minister, the clergy and people of Belgium, awakened to this new phenomenon in their midst. In the blue sky of a perfect August day, aeroplanes were banking as the Press sought for pictures which would report to the world the sights of that tenth birthday of the little curate's work.

To the little curate himself fell the honour he must have coveted above all: to read to the vast assembly, in French and in Flemish, the letter which his friend in Rome, Pope Pius XI, had sent to the Cardinal of Malines for the occasion.

If our heart [the Pope wrote] is not spared many sufferings, it is also given great happinesses. One such joy you have closely shared, dear son, you who have watched the happy birth in your country of this association, today so evidently prospering, which, with its chosen bishops and priests, is to take part in this Congress.

Ten years have passed since the Association of the Young Christian Workers saw the light of day, born in your land with such happy omens. As today we pause to look back along the way it has trodden and consider the great and admirable work it has accomplished, how much it has owed to the power of God who deigned to smile on its work cannot be denied. . . .

Nor could it have been otherwise, given that it is an authentic form of Catholic Action suited to the present times; given, too, that, following the pressing counsels of our mother the Church, it has consecrated all its interests and efforts to the working class which so often is crushed under the weight of misery and deceived by misleading errors. . . .

It is their own daily work which enables them to offer themselves to God as atoning victims and which opens out before them a great field wherein they can realise their longing to bring back their fellow-workers, their brothers, to the practice of the Christian life. We are not without a full knowledge of the way in which, by their devotion, their prayers, their resort to the sacraments, their gentleness and their constant efforts, they seek to win their brothers to Christ as true sources of light, co-workers with the Holy Spirit and front-rank soldiers of the Church.

'An authentic form of Catholic Action'—these were official words of approval at the highest level which no one could gainsay.

In their formations, nine miles long, and carrying 2,000 flags, the Jocists made their way from the religious ceremony in the middle of the day to the great Heysel Stadium where in numbers exceeding the normal capacity of the great stadium, they squeezed themselves into every nook and corner of the amphitheatre. 'Ten years ago, Jocists, how many were you?' a voice shouted. 'Less than five hundred,' the crowd answered. 'And today?'—'A hundred thousand.' —'How many will you be tomorrow?'—'Millions,' they cried.

But it was not to be a night of speeches. The J.O.C. was only to make one—and that a speech in mime. In three parts, the mime enacted, first, the revolt of the workers invoking the use of force against their oppressors and the true answer that nothing would solve the workers' problems but to establish in men's minds the dignity and rights of labour; second, the unemployed, driven to hatred by hunger and despair, hearing the words of Christ and the teaching of the social encyclicals; and, third, the demonstration of the Jocist principles delivering the workers from their sufferings. And the evening ended in an atmosphere of intense enthusiasm with mass demonstration and cries for the coming of the reign of Christ.

National temperaments differ, and it must be confessed that the Anglo-Saxon mind, more moved by understatement than overstatement, might not have felt entirely happy on such an occasion. But Cardijn's mind and temperament are very Continental and he who, in this mood, foresaw 'acts of daring and successes that would astonish the world' certainly felt no remorse at such an appeal to mass-feelings. It should also be remembered how deep was the sense of crisis in the world at that time. In the very different atmosphere of the study conference which began next morning, Cardinal Van Roey said:

> The world is at this moment within the grip of the power of evil as it has rarely been in history. The moral and social order is shaken to its foundations. Whole nations are in the grip of destroying and perverse forces. The cult of materialism is prevailing. We are witnessing a veritable renaissance of ancient paganism in ideas, in morals, in the conception and practice of individual, domestic and social life. Russian Bolshevism, German Nazism, are nothing else, while in every country, ours included, certain parties, certain groups, have as their main purpose the complete dechristianisation of the masses, the brutal and total suppression of all the spiritual riches of humanity.[1]

The challenge of the Y.C.W. demonstration to the current ideas, of which it can at least be certainly said that their consquences were the catastrophe of the Second World War, can hardly have been called in retrospect exaggerated, though, in fact, the movement was destined not to win its way through by such public propaganda but by the unsung hard work of its members, little by little changing the moral and spiritual climate in factory and workshop according to the practical applications of Cardijn's teaching as it best suited their environment and their particular people's

---

[1] The full report of the speeches is to be found in the 374 pages of *Semaine d'Études Internationale*.

mentality. Cardijn himself expressed the real point in his famous 'See, Judge, and Act'—a formula that was neatly to sum up all that he had been saying for twenty years.

> Leaders and members learning to SEE, to JUDGE and to ACT: to SEE the problem of their temporal and eternal destiny; to JUDGE the present situation, the problems, the contradictions, all that is involved and demanded in view of that temporal and eternal destiny; to ACT in view of the conquest of that temporal and eternal destiny. To ACT individually and together, as a team, in the local section, in the regional federation, in a national movement, in meetings, through practical accomplishment, both in individual lives and within the whole *milieu*, thus forming a single front, going forward to conquer on behalf of the masses of the workers, their brothers.

But it was not from Cardijn, but from Cardinal Verdier himself, speaking to priest-chaplains, that some of the shrewdest and most moving words came:

> Yesterday I understood better than ever what Jocism is. It is all in two propositions, I think: 'Never to separate religion from professional life' and from now onwards always to have recourse in every field to 'the apostolate of like by like' . . . Perhaps in the past we have made of religion a kind of flower which we cultivated for ourselves, but after having torn it from its stem. . . . We must work not only for the eternal happiness of men, but also for their temporal happiness. . . . We must also accept that apostolate of like by like. Here is a point which I have to make with a certain degree of feeling where my fellow priests are concerned. I know that your ministry within Jocism is a delicate one, because it must be a hidden one—in a certain measure it must be subordinate to the laity itself. But remembering that, though the heart of man is hidden, it is none the less the source of all life, you will gladly accept your duty of remaining hidden, if I may dare to say so, before these dear children so that they, more freely and maybe in a closer spirit, can be in touch with the worker and decisively influence him.

These were Cardijn's sentiments, but they came with all the more force from a cardinal archbishop.

The chief note of this first international congress was naturally an inquiry into religious and social conditions in the different countries where the movement had already penetrated or was making its first contacts, together with discussion as to how the Jocist method should adapt itself to the new situations. Because of this, the findings of the congress afford us an accurate picture of the spread of the Y.C.W. by 1935.

By that date, apart from Belgium itself and France, Cardijn's movement had established itself in Portugal, Switzerland and Spain and, across the Atlantic, in Canada and Colombia. All progress-reports of the movement, then and now, have to be read with discernment. The Y.C.W. is not a movement which lends itself to easy statistical records since its essential criterion is quality and variety of progress rather than numbers. Y.C.W. sections and regions, with the right chaplains and the right leaders, making their Christian and social influence really felt in their environment, are worth far more to it than large numbers of nominal recruits whose activity consists more in promoting their own external Christian observance than in coming to grips with the social situation around them, and in apostolically influencing those with whom their workers' life is cast. Again, it is easy to step up numbers if a rough count is made of all who have been attracted to the movement at the level of sections, for the section is open to anyone interested. It must be added, further, that the international organisation of the Y.C.W. is, edifyingly, uninterested in statistics, having more important work to do. All that one can say of its rough figures is that they are calculated with extreme conservatism and certainly only include those who formally enter the movement and keep up their subscriptions.

It was Cardijn himself who, during this congress, gave

the briefest of reports of the progress of the movement in Belgium. He said that the four Belgian organisations (Flemish and Walloon for the men and Flemish and Walloon for the girls) had 'despite unemployment and the economic crisis, 80,000 subscribing members, grouped in 2,000 local sections and united into seventy regional federations'. He went on:

> In order to train and enlarge this army and methodically organise its march forward, we have about 150 paid propagandists and 6,000 leaders. These figures mean little, however, in comparison with the daily activity of the movement and its unparalleled influence on the lives and the family and professional *milieu* of the young workers. It constitutes a forward marching dynamism that is capable of renewing the face both of the Church and of our society. Yes, I am an optimist, but a realistic optimist, for I base myself on twenty-nine years of priestly apostolate. Often I say to myself that we priests have little idea of the lay apostolic resources in the hands of the Church, nor do we understand how those resources should be made use of.

The record for France was given by the Abbé Guérin, and his sober account already suggests what constantly strikes the outside observer, namely that France, where the work of permeating the social field with up-to-date religious influences started late and with some uncertainty, was to prove the country where Y.C.W. influence would be the most fruitful in quality and quantity.

> An organisation of young workers, created by the young workers themselves [Abbé Guérin said], has taken in hand the defence of the material and moral interests of wage-earning youth even in the least important industrial regions. A few figures give an idea of the stages of our progress. Since 1927, the number of Jocist sections has risen from six to 1,400. The two movements (male and female) contain 52,000 Jocists who are in touch at the present moment with 100,000 young

workers. The *Jeunesse Ouvrière* and the *Jeunesse Ouvrière Féminine*, our two propaganda papers, have a circulation of about 100,000 each. In seven years the J.O.C. of France has established an organisation for preparing young folk for their working life which covers 15,000 schoolboys and schoolgirls [this corresponds to what in Anglo-Saxon countries is called 'Pre-Y.C.W.']; thrift, military, trade-union, leisure and education services; a national rescue fund for young un-employed which provides money and meals and finds employment.

And the speaker went on to describe other varieties of work achieved in both the religious and the social field, study-weeks, retreats, days of recollection in the religious field, work for the prevention of accidents, professional orientation, diminution of unemployment in the social. 'Today', he concluded, 'the J.O.C. has established its place among the most important youth organisations of our country.'

The personal interest in the movement of the Cardinal Patriarch of Lisbon (himself the youngest cardinal at the time) and his close relations with Cardijn, who had three times visited him, enabled the movement to be established in what the Portuguese chaplain-general described as 'the catacombs'. Here progress could only be slow, with the accent on quality, but a paper had been founded and the J.O.C.F. already had seventy-five sections.

The Swiss report gave no figures, but it is interesting to read in it the fact that the movement interested the Protes-tants—'some Jocists even are Protestant'. It was also pointed out that 'faithful to the Jocist spirit and methods, our J.O.C. will not resemble that of Belgium, France or anywhere else'.

On the eve of the civil war in Spain the Y.C.W. had been securely established in Catalonia and, in view of the future, the chaplain-general's report of a spiritual re-growth after the years of revolution when socialism in Spain and anarchism in Catalonia gained power over the working class makes interesting reading. 'Our inquiries reveal that not more than three per cent. of the workers practise their religion. The priest is avoided, the religious are hated; but a certain degree of religious feeling, stubbornly ignored, remains deep down in people's hearts.' Of the Y.C.W. he said: 'As to results—well we were only born yesterday. Three years ago we began the movement. Besides the few thousands of young people in our ranks, I would like to tell you of one thing achieved. We have created a new type of young worker, fully, joyfully and proudly Christian, who feels, above all, the need to conquer for Christ the world of work.' Dark days were to come before the Y.C.W. could carry out its mission in Spain in very different conditions, but even then not wholly favourable ones, for the free-speech and action on which the movement depends were to be forbidden.

Overseas, the president of the Y.C.W. in Colombia told the only too frequently repeated tale in Latin countries of the advances of anti-clerical socialism in default of any Catholic social organisation. 'Before Jocism, no one was interested in working youth. Whatever was done was done for young students.' It was at the end of December 1932 that the Y.C.W. was started in Bogota and was gradually extended to other centres. Small as it was, with but 1,000 members, the crying need for it in a country where clergy and people had hardly become aware of the social apostolate gave the opportunity of doing solid work far beyond what numbers might lead one to expect.

But in the New World, the country destined to found a Jocist movement comparable with Belgium and France was without question Canada. In three years, nineteen diocesan federations and 172 local sections had been established and they embraced over 6,000 members. Backed by a strong Jocist press, these pioneers, men and women, had

made contact with many more than their own numbers
and 10,000 people attended their first General Council.
They had even established their first colony in the United
States itself. 'The founder of the first Canadian section,'
said the spokesman for Canada, 'is in close relation with the
Founder of Jocism itself, Canon Cardijn. "There can only be
one Jocism: M. Cardijn's" was his constant theme. From
the humblest beginnings great things have come to pass.
Today, its strong organisation covers young workers, men
and women, in large numbers within four of the nine
provinces of Canada.'

Apart from these countries where the Y.C.W. had
definitely started, the International Jubilee Congress heard
reports of detailed social and worker conditions for youth,
as well as of existing movements to improve them, from
delegates of Holland, Luxemburg, Denmark, Poland, Yugo-
slavia, China, and from 'the Africa which awaits you'.

The reports, as one reads them today, are astonishingly
impressive in that they themselves are so clearly the fruit
of the Y.C.W. inquiry method—the first word of the 'See,
Judge, Act' trilogy. After all, it was only a relatively few
years since the new curate of Laeken had set his uneducated
girl apprentices inquiring into the social conditions under
which they worked and making their practical, concrete
reports. It was only ten years since the movement had been
officially established. And today it was the nations of the
world which were reporting at headquarters about the life
and fate of working youth in environments so distant and
often so strange. For a country like Colombia it was
absolutely virgin soil. No one could doubt that Cardijn's
work had in it the power to develop in a massive way.

The 'new curate' could feel that he had come a long way
as, during those days, he brushed shoulders with his disciples, priest and laymen, from all over the world and noted
the universal enthusiasm for the ideas and the organisation

Since the end of the war Cardijn has helped to spread his movement of Young Christian Workers throughout the world.

*Rom Maione was elected international president of the J.O.C. in 1957.
Born a Canadian, but of Italian stock, he is Cardijn's second English-speaking
right-hand man.*

he had pioneered. To hear Cardijn, to speak to him, to get his advice, was the most prized privilege of those who had come to Brussels. Cardijn, a humble man of God, did not attribute all this manifest evidence of success to himself, and the observer cannot help feeling that in a certain sense he was right, apart from supernatural considerations. For the unfolding of the Y.C.W. was not the work of Cardijn in the sense in which an army owes all to its commander's orders or a party to its political chief; the unfolding was the unfolding of an idea which carried its evolution within it. Having preached the idea and begun the practical work of its realisation where his hands could reach, Cardijn could watch its organic growth and diffusion in a way far more truly 'determinist' because far more rational than the Marxist materialistic dialectic. That had to be forced on to men by agitation, trickery and physical revolt against unbearable conditions. But given priests and leaders of good will who had once understood what Cardijn meant, then an inner spiritual and idealistic compulsion would take over, so long as men awoke to the truth that they were ends in themselves and not mere means for the materialistic ends of small minorities. The biggest danger for him lay in the failure of priests to understand the essential missionary quality of the spiritual aspect of his movement, and more important perhaps than the many eloquent passages in Cardijn's speeches during the days of the Jubilee Congresses were the following, which came incidentally in the course of an address on the J.O.C.F. which he gave to the women: 'We have no use for a sentimental religious piety which lasts a few weeks or even a few days, nor a mawkish piety of superficial practices, nor yet a spirituality to one side of everyday life. We have to win over the whole life of young workers, in their families, their work, their sentiments, so that it all becomes a means of collaboration with God.'

K

9

CARDIJN AND THE Y.C.W. ADAPTED
FOR WAR
(1939-1945)

For twenty years and more Cardijn had been struggling to recall to the masses of forgotten and uprooted men and women what was really involved in the Christian teaching that every person is created in the image of God to achieve a divine destiny. In this he was doing what every pope, every bishop, every priest had been doing for twenty centuries. It was in the light of that fundamental Christian truth that the whole moral teaching of the Church made sense. And indeed for many centuries that teaching had so far governed the political and moral order of Christendom that, for example, it was taken for granted that if a person lived to become rich at the expense of his neighbours, to achieve power over them, and to use his fellow men as mere instruments in the pursuit of his ambitions, he was no better than a common thief and a good deal worse than a common adulterer. The Church could not repress the self-regarding human appetites which in fact, even among popes and churchmen, made men covetous, avaricious and unjust, but it maintained its condemnation of the pursuit of wealth and power for their own sake. But with the division of Christendom after the Reformation, the civilised West gradually came to accept the view that politics and economics had nothing to do with religion and spiritual ideals. Economics was governed in terms of 'economic man' and the pursuit of wealth and power was the duty of the State. At the same time man discovered revolutionary new sources of enrichment and new methods of acquiring, increasing and maintaining power. Totally disregarding spiritual and moral principles as inapplicable to economics and politics, competition and strife came to govern the relations between nations and the relations between man and man in industrial organisation. The inevitable consequence was the emergence of a 'liberal' world of international and class war in which the strong became stronger and the weak weaker.

Horrified by these consequences, many a reformer had sought in one way or another to protect the victims of this jungle world, and many had offered over-all solutions in terms of new ideologies. But protection of the victims was no more than first-aid in a continuing crisis and, at bottom, new ideologies came to no more than trying to ensure absolute power for one or other sets of contestants in the struggle.

The one solution which evaded everyone was the simplest of all: the recognition again of the spiritual nature of each and every man—a spiritual nature resting on the fact that God created every man in his own image, a spiritual nature which imposed on every man inalienable rights and absolute duties. Tragically, even professing Christians, in their post-Reformation weakness, had been elbowed away from the economic, social and political field and had become content to look upon religion as a sectarian or private business of direct relevance only to private and personal lives. Because of this, they even drifted into the view that the disorders of the world with their tragic consequences for the weak were all part of a mysterious providential disposition, to which men had to be resigned as part of the price to be paid for personal salvation in a better world.

It was only in the social encyclicals of modern popes that the world—and even the Christian world—heard again, applied to new conditions, the economic and political teaching which was commonplace in the Middle Ages. Even so, the popes had been heard with grumbling, distaste and disregard. It needed a humble curate of Laeken to realise that the practical way forward could only lie in the long and hard work of actually re-forming Christian consciences so that they could come to see again the intimate link between the Christian spiritual teaching about human nature and destiny and any worthwhile social revolution. Choosing the field of his own natural interest—youth, and youth of the working classes—he undertook to form Christian workers in the temporal and spiritual sense, never doubting that every such 're-formed' Christian worker would be in his life and work a 're-former' of his fellow-workers. From this initiative, this Christian 're-formation', which is what Cardijn means by missionary or militant or apostolic action, has little by little spread within the Church to all kinds of 'specialised Catholic Action', as it is called. It has also indirectly led to fresh ideas in all aspects of Catholic life, liturgy, and formation.

Contrasted with the size of the problem which has to be solved, Cardijn's method, only slowly and in face of opposition accepted by Catholics themselves, had made but infinitesimal progress and reform. But the rightness and ultimate inevitableness of Cardijn's ideas are not affected by the fact that to succeed they must conquer, not a few here and there in the world but a world itself—a world whose social problems with the speedy growth of population and the opening out of new and gigantic industrial territories are increasing rather than diminishing.

In view of all this, it could not be unexpected that just as Cardijn's first lone efforts had been thrust aside by the impact of the first of the world wars which resulted from the secularist disorder of the world, so after ten years of good progress a second world war, expressing far more clearly the world's spiritual and moral bankruptcy, should threaten to destroy all that he had accomplished.

Each year Cardijn lectured at Eastertide to federal leaders of the Y.C.W. during a week's Study Conference at Godinne, and much of what he said on these occasions has been preserved. Working through the pages of his lectures, one comes across passages where his words directly reflect the condition of the times. Thus in 1936 we read:

> In the face of different threatening possibilities, we must avoid spreading a spirit of panic around us. Two extremes should be avoided. We must first avoid false security for Catholics. Do not think that because Catholics are in power all is necessarily well and that things may be allowed to drift. That state of mind has caused formidable ruins in some countries. What a mistake to look only to the labels which political men give themselves and to forget the fate of the people. It would be hard to exaggerate the harm that can be done to the Church through such false security. The other mistake is to think that because a Catholic government loses power, all is lost. The coming of a bad government may prove an excellent trial. Without it, eyes might have remained closed. The words of the Church *felix culpa* can be applicable in this context.[1]

On the same occasion Cardijn asked what should be thought of the new movements—communism, socialism, rexism, nationalism, etc.

> I put them all on the same footing [he said]. We must not allow passion to dictate our attitude. It is a question of the virtue of prudence. . . . I see them as essentially anti-political movements. They destroy politics itself, both in its exercise and in the choosing of politicians and also because they unjustly and unnecessarily influence public opinion in regard to governments. These movements are revolutionary in the

[1] *Godinne* (1936), pp. 41-2.

bad sense of the word, for order is not re-established by force and terror. They are evil-doing and criminal organisations. . . . One may be a genius in criticism and useless in construction. Politics is essentially a constructive and realising art. We must stick closer and closer to our Jocist programme. . . . We must take positive attitudes in the face of the political situation, everyone ready to act loyally right to the very end.[1]

Two years later, at Godinne, Cardijn analysed the background of the situation with the words:

We must realise more and more the greatest error of liberalism and individualism during the nineteenth century. Political rights were given to all citizens. Personal duties were thrust upon them. In a word, citizens were given responsibilities in the life of the State, but everyone forgot the main thing needful, namely to educate them. Liberalism in the nineteenth century laid the foundation for political acts but never afforded the necessary formation. That is why the totalitarian States today are taking their revenge. Cross the frontier over there and see how they attend to the political education of the child, the young man, the adult. But they are doing it all wrong and, anyway, the terror régime destroys all educative value in political formation. That is where the great danger of today lies. Indeed, we can watch it giving rise to formidable events: we see a man, who pretends to be a god, seducing millions upon millions of souls. . . . All this teaches you the need for a Christian political formation in any country. It is necessary for the defence of the Church, and for the religion, morals, social life of the faithful who profit from it for the attaining of their eternal destiny. That is what the J.O.C. has done and goes on doing. For thirteen years we have been responsible for a political formation without knowing it; and my contention is that it is the most necessary of all schools from the fundamental point of view of the groundwork and principles.[2]

Godinne (1936), p. 41.   [2] Ibid. (1938), p. 33.

As so often, Cardijn, accidentally referring to a contemporary subject, finds himself demonstrating yet again how the elements of the Y.C.W. formation involve so very much more than the superficial observer would believe.

In 1939 at Godinne Cardijn began right away with the words:

> The world has reached an impasse. . . . We have reached the end of the period of treasons and downfalls which began hundreds of years ago and which causes us to face today the dilemma: either come back to God or finish it all with war and destruction. Between the alternatives there is no middle way. When they talk to me of war, I say that apostasy is war, that paganism is war. Do you want to save working youth from war? Then save it from apostasy and paganism.

Recounting the meaning and history of apostasy, he said:

> There have always been and there always will be apostates, but today we are watching what the Pope calls the 'apostasy of the masses'. There are whole countries where, with violence and persecution, the attempt is made to kill the very idea of God, God's laws and the worship of God in the soul of the mass of the people. Such has been the history of Russia, of Mexico and, during these last years, the history of a large part of Spain.

Distinguishing such open persecution from others, he continued:

> Apart from such States where millions have been forced to apostatise under threat of persecution, we have today so-called totalitarian States. These aspire to a new conception of life and of national community, but in doing this they cut away from the soul of the people the idea of God, the Sovereign Judge, and from Christ, the Saviour of men. In Germany and in other totalitarian States we see a fashion of educating youth, of organising the State and of spreading an ideology, which must necessarily lead to the apostasy of the masses.[1]

[1] Quotations from the first lesson of *Godinne* (1939).

And Cardijn's analysis of the situation, as with any analysis if it proceeds from fundamental Christian principles, did not spare the constitutional and free countries.

Then there are the free countries like Belgium, France, England, the United States and most countries in the world. In these an unconscious, anonymous apostasy began with liberalism. First, earthly life and its organisation were separated from the idea of God and his authority and from religion. Then the pretence was made that the State, together with its public and private institutions, should be neutral. God, religion and the eternal truths were not the State's business. These basic and eternal realities were only a matter for private consciences, and their application to the present life, individual, family, professional, national and international, was of no concern to the State. Under the influence of liberalism, materialism, pleasure, distraction, fun, the masses have been slowly led away so that we have reached a state in the world of which it may be said that apostasy threatens to become general.

And Cardijn went on to show that the inevitable effect of such apostasy among the masses is the creation of a new paganism and a new religion worshipping false gods.

Do not believe that technocracy and technical progress enable man to do without ideals. On the contrary! The worship of Reason, of Liberty, Fraternity and Equality, of Science, of Beauty has been proposed to some. To others today the cult of blood, race and national community is offered. This cult is concretised in a single man who has become the incarnation, the personification of race and national community. He is held to be a god. He cannot err himself nor deceive the people. They follow him not because he represents God, but because he is the people incarnate. It is this most dangerous of idolatries which is now threatening contemporary civilisation.[1]

[1] Quotations from the first lesson of *Godinne* (1939).

Later, he turned to another aspect of the world situation which he roundly dubbed 'an abominable crime' in that thousands of millions were being spent on armaments while millions were suffering hunger and cold. 'We are spending thousands of millions in order to make the world today a fortified camp and tomorrow an immense cemetery.'[1]

Cardijn was prophesying only too accurately, but, as with so many others at the time, despair itself brought forth the last hopes of yet avoiding disaster. He planned a great pilgrimage of Christian youth to Rome. He called on his young apostles in their factories and workshops, in their homes, in the streets, in their free time to work to save their brothers from what seemed inevitable. The pilgrimage to Rome would show to the working classes and to the world the need of the Y.C.W. apostolate, if the peace of the world was to be saved.

> We must multiply meetings to explain the meaning of our pilgrimage—meetings against war and for peace; meetings in which thousands of young workers will carry the Cross on which Christ died to save the world. An irresistible offensive is needed to draw the working class into preparation for this pilgrimage and this crusade for peace. Thus we shall establish in all countries the single front of the young workers represented by thousands of delegates before the visible representative of the only Prince of Peace.[2]

Cardijn's last hope and prayer for peace was planned and organised on a massive scale. Twenty countries from the old world and the new would be represented. Twenty thousand delegates would descend on Rome, where within the Vatican Palace itself an international congress of working youth would be held. All was arranged and ready—for the fatal month of September. Perhaps in his great disappointment Cardijn recalled the words he spoke at the 1937 Y.C.W. congress in Paris where 80,000 Jocists filled

[1] Ibid.   [2] Ibid.

the Parc des Princes, with five cardinals and thirty bishops present. 'Jocists,' he said to the great gathering, 'to save the working class of your country, Christ will need apostles. You shall be the apostles. He will need saints. You shall be the saints. He will need martyrs. You shall be the martyrs.'[1]

The pilgrims of peace were to face the martyrdom of war, and not a few of them were to be martyrs indeed for their principles, including two of the original three musketeers.

Cardijn's insistence that Jocism is a principle of apostolate—in essence *the* principle of lay apostolate—was quickly borne out when the Second World War began. Automatically and inevitably, Jocism adapted itself to the new conditions. 'We shall now work for the young mobilised workers and leave it till after the war to go to Rome.' Many thousands of Jocists were mobilised into the French army, where they carried on their work of being good Christians in being good soldiers, much of the Jocist life continuing in camps and on the Maginot Line, while those who remained behind did all they could to help families whose breadwinner was away.

But it was after the Germans launched their great offensive in May 1940 that the full wartime resources of the movement were seen. For the Y.C.W., as for everyone else in the threatened lands, the question of whether to stay at home or to fly the country presented itself. Jocism, in effect, divided itself and was thus able to help look after and comfort those who felt it their duty to stay, while also protecting and aiding the pitiful masses who fled before the oncoming enemy, gathering about them all that they could carry, and defending themselves as best they could from the cruel attacks by aircraft. Cardijn himself foresaw the immense work which the settlement of these masses of refugees would demand, both spiritually and temporally, and soon he was everywhere in France, helping to organise

[1] *Cardijn*, op. cit., p. 33.

accommodation and settlement for the thousands of young people, whether within the military forces or out of them, so that the least spiritual and temporal harm might be done to them in these appalling conditions. In some cases it was due to him that grave disorders were avoided or minimised. He travelled from one town to another all over the country, and exerted himself to the utmost of his capacity to organise some spiritual ministration for young soldiers and young lay people, appealing in the papers for priests to volunteer for this essential work. In the south he worked in co-operation with Cardinal Saliège, Archbishop of Toulouse, and preached for the cause in the Cardinal's cathedral. He realised better than others that just as war is fought by youth so the effects of wholesale movement of masses and consequent social disorganisation can do graver injuries to young people, deprived of leaders and family ties, than to others. Whole future lives might be at stake in so terrible an experience. Belgian and French Jocists had become one in the hour of trial and suffering and under their founder they performed prodigies for the care of the uprooted youth.

But the war pursued its relentless and disastrous course. Within a few weeks, resistance in Europe was over, and with the capitulation and armistice totally new conditions faced the movement.

Under Nazi occupation it was not to be expected that the virile J.O.C. could continue its normal work unmolested. In occupied territory it had to be secret; elsewhere it supported 'Moral Resistance' against Nazification. It is interesting here to notice that a movement so soundly based on Christian principles was never faced as such with the dilemma of resistance or collaboration. Individuals within it might have to make that choice, but the movement as such in living up to its ideals carried on its work as best it could and where it could, ready to resist the moment anything was demanded of it incompatible with its spiritual duties and temporal action springing from Christian patriotism and, above all, incompatible with that charity and love of country and neighbours which spring from the Gospels. Its martyrs and its wounded were not, as we shall see, the result of flamboyant action, but of determination to follow the course of duty and painfully accept whatever might result from such determination.

In Cardijn's words at Godinne in 1941, the movement had 'to go into retreat'—not a physical retreat, but a spiritual retreat, so that its spiritual basis might be deepened and a fuller understanding gained of all that the suffering around them truly meant.

> We must inspire [he said] a *mystique* of action which can move working youth—an offensive action, not a defensive one. The J.O.C. is not a Maginot Line, but an army of the air, a motorised, tank formation. Action in full living, in the fullness of circumstances, in the centre of the mass. To do this, the J.O.C. must learn to work through personal action, through collective action, influential and conquering, educative action which forms and toughens, in perfect and well-finished actions, well prepared and continuous; in action within and outside the Movement.[1]

The formula, it will be seen, was far-reaching, yet it could be lived in any conditions, even those of Nazi occupation. Belgium and France (which managed to celebrate the J.O.C.'s fifteenth anniversary) in those days offered endless opportunities for every kind of action, helping to reunite families, feeding and housing refugees and collecting for their material needs, organising welcome centres, keeping in touch with prisoners of war and deported workers, preparing for the future. None of this work was exclusive to Cardijn's movement of course, but in its case the spirit and purpose of the movement remained the directing force. It was always the apostolate of youth; the handing over of

[1] *Godinne* (1941), p. 12.

responsibility to youth; and, not least, the constant fact-finding which, in these conditions, so much enriched the intellectual and moral capital of the movement.

Cardijn was under no illusions about the future. He prefaced the Woluwe leaders' study week of 1942 with the warning that the meeting would be held 'at a moment especially grave for the Church and for the world. What is happening around us today is deciding the fate of millions of men and, indeed, of the greater part of mankind.'[1] Later in the same study week he said:

The present transformations of society and the conditions of life that will follow from the war, so far from weakening our ardour and courage in defending and saving the dignity of the worker, must on the contrary inspire and increase tenfold a Christian heroism in the struggle and conquest for the personal dignity of every young worker. Just as the early Christians, so far from letting themselves be depressed by the power and domination of a paganism which caused slavery, idolatry and barbarism to flourish, succeeded by their example, their influence and their conquests at the heart of contemporary life in overcoming paganism and transforming a pagan civilisation and ethos into a Christian one, so must we. The J.O.C. must form and multiply the Christians of the new times. . . . Everything must be made ready, here and now, whatever the outcome of the war: (*a*) society must not return to the fallacies of liberalism and individualism, abandoning youth in its educational and post-educational period; (*b*) society must not be lured into an incomplete, false and disastrous bringing-up of youth; (*c*) society must be furnished with a régime of education which will make men understand, appreciate, will and realise the dignity of the human person, human destiny and human vocation among all young workers.

And Cardijn showed in detail how the against the background of the work imposed upon the movement in the

[1] *Woluwe* (1942), p. 2.

conditions of occupation, the formation of young Christian
youth could continue and develop against a background of
'a deep sense of national pride and solidarity, patriotic
devotion and heroic fidelity to the historic mission of the
Belgian people'.[1]

It all sounded easy on paper. In fact, of course, it
continuously imperilled the leaders of the movement and
well-known people closely associated with it, for if not a
movement of physical resistance to the occupying power, it
was a movement of spiritual resistance with all that this
must entail in the temporal order. It followed that behind
the scenes the J.O.C. proved to be not only a focus and
spiritual and moral support and uplift against the anti-
Christian philosophy of Nazism within Belgium, but Jocist
sections to the number of over 600 were secretly created
among worker deportees in Germany and Austria right up
to the Soviet borders. In Belgium study meetings and other
activities of the movement were often held under the
appearance of gymnastic and other normal youth work,
and Cardijn himself, who because of his reputation had to
move with caution, was, on one occasion, taken secretly to
a leaders' study week. The size of the meeting aroused the
suspicion of the Gestapo, which paid it a visit but considered the Canon's papers sufficiently in order. Such
meetings, however, could not be safely continued. Naturally, far greater precautions were necessary in enemy
country. Nevertheless, the deportee worker Jocists of
Belgium, France and elsewhere managed to have a national
secretariat at work in Berlin itself, to issue a secret bulletin,
and even to secrete a Jocist flag which was set up when
sections met and prayed together. The versatility of the
Y.C.W. in such different and apparently impossible conditions was an eloquent sign of its vitality and inspiration.

There can be little doubt that the German authorities

[1] *Woluwe* (1942), pp. 13–14.

would have made short work of Cardijn and other Y.C.W. leaders in Belgium but for their fear of the influence over the people of the Church and its leader Cardinal Van Roey. As it was, they did arrest Cardijn and some others in 1942 on a charge of his having denounced the deportation of young workers to German factories. Once again, the founder found himself in the prison of Saint-Gilles, this time in a little cell which he had to share with socialists and communists. It was an opportunity for him to get through some homework in the shape of studying the texts of Rosenberg and Karl Marx. How often his mind must have gone back to that first imprisonment when, as a still young curate, he was working out the principles and practice of a young workers' movement which might or might not be realised in the way he dreamt. Now, in the darkest hour for the world around him, he at least could have had no doubt about the worth of what he had effected and about the future development, come what might, of the movement which Pius XI had taken to his heart and which had grown to undreamt-of international proportions. The Y.C.W., under the baptism of Rosenberg's and Marx's fires, was not only surviving, but, in Canon Cardijn's favourite word, 'conquering' even in the heart of enemy country and adapting itself to home needs in exactly the way so dynamic and comprehensive a movement should. Its possible scope seemed unlimited. It was changing the missionary concept of the Church in modern times.

Cardijn's imprisonment was short, for the German authorities were afraid of offending the Cardinal and doubtless hoping to woo him. After three months, he was released. He used his own imprisonment and his release to good purpose as a lever to force the Germans to free his friends imprisoned with him. Daily, Cardijn insisted on going to the authorities and demanding their release on the ground that they had been imprisoned for the same reasons as himself. 'If you do not let them go, I shall go back to Saint-Gilles myself,' he threatened them. And they had to give way. All this was typical of the solidarity of the movement under war conditions. Their thoughts and prayers were always with one another, not least with the victims of war, whether in the prison-camps or in enemy factories where they were forced to work against the interests of their country and their movement. In France, Abbé Guérin was imprisoned in Fresnes, the headquarters seized, and a number of Jocists shot or sent to concentration camps.

Tonnet, Garcet, and other leaders whose lives had been so closely associated with the story of Cardijn's movement were carrying on in every way possible their apostolic vocation in helping all who were suffering at home and abroad from the consequences of war and occupation. They had behaved with caution and had so far remained unmolested. In the end, it was not by any heroic act of defiance, but in what might be called thes imple down-to-earth Jocist way, that tragedy came to Fernand Tonnet and Paul Garcet, the first two musketeers. As with many thousands of others in Belgium, Holland, France, Norway, Paul Garcet did not hesitate one day in 1943 about his personal duty when it was a question of helping an Allied parachutist, and Tonnet was in the secret. Garcet was arrested. Tonnet knew that it would not be long before the German secret police would be on to him as an accomplice, or at any rate as having failed to report the matter to the authorities. He was soon taken for questioning, and though he could not deny his knowledge, he was released. But he thoroughly understood that the reprieve would not last, and quietly he made his preparations for the arrest which would bring him close again to his dearest lifelong friend, Paul Garcet. So it happened.

Tonnet, quiet, saintly, a man who could not but do good, was arrested on 10 August 1943. With Paul he was soon

Africans at the J.O.C. international congress in Rome.

St. Peter's Square in Rome during a mime given by the J.O.C. at their congress.

Mgr. Cardijn and Pat Keegan at the grave of Mahatma Gandhi.

Mgr. Cardijn at a meeting in a schoolroom at Warrington, Lancs.

taken from Saint-Gilles to the concentration camp of Esterwegen, where they were both classified *Nacht und Nebel*, that is, belonging to the night and the clouds—not to be seen or heard of again. Nor were they the only Jocists in the camp. From Esterwegen to Bayreuth after seven months. From Bayreuth to dreaded Dachau in the winter of 1944. There, as day by day they grew weaker with hunger and illness, they formed part of a Christian community recalling the life of the catacombs, even to the distribution of the Blessed Sacrament in a little medicine tin to their companions on the rare occasions when a priest could say Mass. In the freezing cold conditions of hard winter, Paul Garcet grew weaker and weaker, and on 23 January he died, as Fernand, himself at death's door, sat by the bedside. A week later, Fernand Tonnet shared his great friend's supreme escape from those months of living death. It was surely in keeping with the whole inner spirit of Cardijn's movement that these first disciples of his should share the martyrdom of the hundreds of thousands thus callously sacrificed in the cause of the Nazi revolt against all the principles of dignified, human Christian life for which their leader had been labouring for over fifty years. This martyrdom was an example of the true cost which the spirit of the Y.C.W. in the contemporary pagan world demanded. They carried in full measure the true burden which others were spared.[1]

And what of their founder himself? Was he to be spared? Mysteriously, it seemed so, despite the ever-growing desperateness of the Germans, facing days of imminent and overwhelming defeat as the Allies swept forward north-west in the late summer of 1944. His activities were well-known. The moral strength he afforded his fellow-countrymen was obvious. To have him in their power would be a valuable asset as the Nazis were evacuating Belgium.

[1] The whole moving story is fully described in Mlle Fièvez's *Fernand Tonnet*.

L

The days passed and it was only in the early morning of 3 September when the last of the Germans were leaving Brussels, that day to be formally liberated, that heavy knocking was heard at the tough door of 97 Rue des Palais, the old J.O.C. International, now the Chaplain-General's home. Sixteen German police were there, seeking hostages and intent on taking with them Canon Cardijn himself, a rich revenge and a valuable prize. Cardijn was at that moment vesting and getting ready to celebrate Mass in the little ground-floor chapel. Before the Germans could enter, he was warned. Quickly, he rushed up the steep and long staircase, climbed up on to the roof and made his way behind a tall chimney stack on a neighbouring house. The Germans searched thoroughly inside the big house, but in their hurry did not climb on to the roof. Satisfied that Cardijn could not be at home, they left. Cardijn quietly re-entered, went down the staircase and re-entered the chapel. In a moment, he was starting his Mass, doubtless of thanksgiving. In fact, had the Germans found him, no more would ever have been heard of him, for such was the fate of other hostages captured that day.

It had been a close thing—and a providential escape from the martyrdom suffered by his lay comrades, Fernand and Paul. But it would be wrong to suppose that Cardijn, in being spared the horrors of the concentration camp, had been spared long moments of suffering. Canon Guérin, of the French Y.C.W., has written:

> Mgr. Cardijn has given his life for the world apostolate. Commissioned by the Hierarchy, he has lived the life of that Movement 'upon which Providence itself has put its signature'. He has had to suffer greatly if I may judge by my own experience, for when one is deeply engaged in a work as he has been for so many years, one feels intensely defections, difficulties, indifference on the part of those without whom one cannot make progress—one suffers, too, from unjust criticisms.

I can well imagine what Joseph Cardijn has felt and suffered. To be committed to such a point in a work of this kind, believe me, means the Cross—and through the Cross the fruitfulness of the apostolate.[1]

It would take a much longer book to describe the details and stories of how Cardijn and the Y.C.W. lived in danger through those years of war, how they lived in anxiety for their fellow-workers and their followers, uncertain of the issues of the war, certain at heart—for Cardijn, however optimistic, was a hard-headed Flemish realist—that war in itself, however it ended, could in itself bring no good, but on the contrary fresh troubles, fresh difficulties, a recrudescence of the paganism which he so detested because it lessened the status and dignity of man and of the worker in particular. The Y.C.W., once so nearly lost—and what suffering those moments must have meant to Cardijn as all his hopes rested on the welcome given by a Pope to a humble Belgian curate—was safe; but it was not the fame or size of the Y.C.W. which interested its founder; it was the degree of work it could accomplish for the cause he had had at heart from the beginning: the raising of the human and spiritual status of the young worker through his own realisation that he was created in God's image to live in this world a life that did not deny and insult the divine spark within him. It is not in times of reaction from the sufferings, efforts and dangers of war that men, whether workers or employers, poor or rich, young or old, most easily remember that they are divinely-created human beings, not just animals to be well-fed, to indulge their passions, to live by forgetfulness of self in the escape of amusement and ditraction. The post-war future of the Y.C.W. would have its many disappointments as well as its great successes.

[1] *Notes de Pastorale Jociste*, Aug.–Sept. 1956, p. 177.

IO

A NAME TO CONJURE WITH ALL THE WORLD OVER

WITH the ending of hostilities, Cardijn realised as fully as others that a new world had to be built, but for him it was not just a case of finding technical solutions to technical problems so that a world of peace and plenty could be established. Almost his first words were: 'The whole world and especially the world of the workers, is threatened by an unprecedented crisis of materialism.'

Jocists in Belgium, France and other occupied countries hardly shared the general optimism. Trained to look beyond materialist appearances they were a little disheartened to see what had happened to the minds of men.

> The war [Cardijn said] has upset the spirit of people and brought about changes in ideas and morals. Privations of war, the nerve-strain through bombing, living in hiding, life in the *maquis*, in prison camps and under deportation conditions—all this contrasted with sudden liberation has caused an explosion of joy easy enough to understand, but also a *détente* that has increasingly expressed itself in a loosening of moral principles. This drive towards pleasure and joy, accompanied as it has been with a lessening of religious sense, has become general and affected all strata of society.[1]

For him, therefore, the task of the movement, so far from lessening, had enormously increased. His lifelong conviction that social justice and human happiness for the workers

[1] *Rapport d'Activité* (1944–46), p. 1.

could only be built on a realisation of the dignity and responsibilities of every person created in God's image, meant
that he was under absolutely no illusions about any world
future which disregarded that truth.

> That is why [he said], the task of the Y.C.W. is clearly more
> urgent and more necessary than ever. While fighting to
> obtain more human conditions of life for the young workers
> of all countries, the Y.C.W. must enable these young people
> to realise the dignity of man as a son of God and to help him
> towards a higher sense of his life as a person and his life as a
> Christian more deeply lived in a manner worthy of his
> eternal destiny.[1]

Happily and yet unhappily, the year of the ending of the
war coincided with the twentieth anniversary of the foundation of the J.O.C.—unhappily, because Canon Cardijn had
always believed in the value to the movement of the com-
memoration on a massive scale of such stages on its way
forward. Memories of the celebrations in 1935 remained
vivid, for the five years of war seemed like an interlude best
forgotten in the immediate aftermath of war and suffering,
however valuable spiritually and as a school of bitter
experience. Circumstances made it now impossible to repeat them on the scale they deserved. But it was also a
happy coincidence, since the twentieth anniversary was an
occasion both for studying the problems of the future and
for an international gathering which could organise the
movement internationally for a world whose problems and
whose sense was becoming ever more international.

In effect the aniversary was celebrated in the Cirque
Royal on 25 July by a gathering of some 12,000 leaders
from Belgium itself and by the organisation of 165 regional
conferences through which some 300,000 young Belgian
workers had the opportunity of regaining the sense of

[1] Ibid., p. 2.

Christian worker-youth solidarity of which they had been deprived during the years of war. But more important was the fact that despite the difficulties of travel in the immediate aftermath of war the occasion also took on an international character. From France, Canada, America and England small delegations came and, in view of the problems of the future, the International Secretariat of the Y.C.W. was established. This was the first occasion on which England was officially represented, for the Y.C.W. had been established in Wigan and London in 1937, the small English Y.C.W. being destined to produce Pat Keegan, International Secretary and International President and one of the closest co-workers with Cardijn in the post-war years. It had even attracted, as we have seen, the attention by that date of the Church of England through a paper read by the Abbé Kothen, Canon Cardijn's deputy, at a Summer School of Sociology, and an experimental Y.C.W. called the Christian Workers' Union was started in Sheffield.

Post-war times would not allow the re-planning of the great pilgrimage to Rome which Cardijn and the Y.C.W. were preparing on the eve of the war, but no duty was more pressing for the founder of the movement than to make contact with Pius XII, acquaint him personally with the record of the Y.C.W. during the years of war, and obtain his personal approval and blessing as the movement began its task of facing up to the immense post-war social problems of youth.

With the international delegates, therefore, Cardijn journeyed to Rome. Pius XII was better aware than anyone of the changes which had come over the world and in particular of the sense of working-class and democratic emancipation which was so strongly felt in Europe in the hour of victory over Nazism and Fascism and while the honeymoon, disturbed as it had already become, with the

Soviet ally was still in being. Against this background the new Pope must have been even more disposed than his predecessor to welcome a visitor who had made it his life's work to raise the status and defend the rights of worker-youth on the only basis which could give real hope to the workers and to the world—the basis of the spiritual and temporal dignity of every human being. Cardijn's mind and the new Pope's were very close together.

Cardijn, indeed, was now received in Rome and at the Vatican like an ambassador of the young working peoples of the world in whom the future of the world so largely rested. Embraced by the Pope, he was bidden to tell about the fortunes and experiences of the movement in the dark years, and the Pope was deeply moved by the wonderful story of how in enemy and occupied countries the Young Christian Workers had bravely carried on with their apostolic mission and their Christian responsibilities to their fellow-workers. 'But they are truly confessors of the Faith,' the Holy Father exclaimed. The Pope was entirely in agreement with Cardijn's whole approach to the contemporary problem of true worker-emancipation in a world more materialistic than ever and with the shadow of Moscow falling across the map of the West.

'The greatest danger for the Church,' Pius XII said to Cardijn, 'is neither communism nor socialism; the greatest danger to the Church lies in the fact that the working class does not understand the teaching of the Church about the working class.'

Cardijn, thinking doubtless of this conversation with the Supreme Pontiff, was to say a little later:

> The working class is unaware of its divine mission. That is why anti-communism is not enough to save the working class and the Church. Nazis, fascists, capitalists know all about anti-communism and they willingly pull out that stop. I have read books on communism and refutations of communism

and many of them refute its errors ably. But what is forgotten is the basic point of communism. People forget that element of truth which is the strength of communism. It is that Marx and communism are giving the working class a mission. Marx says: the working class has a divine mission to fulfil on this earth. That is why he cried: 'Proletariat of the world, unite!' You have a divine mission: you are the redeemers of the world, you, the working class. You are the class which must redeem the world of its sins. In this claim there is a big element of truth. But communism denies God and makes a god of the working class; it denies Christ and makes a christ of the working class. And then it gives it a mission of dictatorship, of force, in order to liberate the people and the world from error and sin. There is in Marxism an element of truth which is a formidable danger and one not sufficiently considered. That danger is the redemptive and messianic mission of Marxism. It is a real worker-mission. The Pope has explained all this in his encyclical. Alas, the negative part of what he says is studied, not the positive part. Those who read *Divini Redemptoris* stop short at the refutations of communism. But the greater part of the encyclical dwells on what must be done in order to go beyond and replace communism. People are silent about all that.[1]

In Rome Cardijn was called upon to give lectures and explanations, in the presence of the highest ecclesiastical officials, of the principles of the Y.C.W. and the missionary lay apostolate which had borne such visible proof, conforming as it so patently did with the needs of the Church and the world in the critical days ahead. And the Pope, blessing the movement as the proper type of Christian answer to the great communist and pagan threat to the workers of the world, sent Cardijn a personally signed letter of congratulations and advocacy of the principles of the movement in which he said: 'At this moment when a new world is arising on the ruins of a merciless war, we cannot but express

[1] *L'Heure de la Classe Ouvrière* (1948), pp. 18–19.

our ardent hopes that the law of Christ our Lord should triumph in all sections of society as among all nations, and especially thanks to the providential working of the Y.C.W. among the working masses of Belgium and other countries.'

But in these immediate post-war days of the movement's history there is perhaps nothing more significant than a small detail. After the visit to Rome, and thus commissioned by Pius XII to be in the vanguard of the Church's crusade to win back the disorientated world for Christ by fighting to create an intrinsically better and more dignified world, as much in the temporal as in the spiritual sense— and to do this by forming responsible lay apostles or missionaries who were better at their worldly job than others—Cardijn determined to gather together Y.C.W. leaders from as many countries as possible to study the whole problem. To this meeting were invited Y.C.W. delegates from the ex-enemy countries of Germany and Austria, a small and perhaps even inevitable development. But in the generous and sincere welcome given to Germans of whom it had so lately been said, even by reasonable people calling themselves Christian, that 'the only good German was the dead one', a facet of the Cardijn's movement, not perhaps sufficiently underlined, was vividly illustrated.

The young Cardijn had felt himself to have close ties with Germany, and the 1914 invasion came as a personal blow to him. Twice he and his fellow Belgians had suffered bitterly at German hands and, in between the wars, Germany had worshipped a totalitarian ideal of materialistic force utterly revolting to him. But through all this Cardijn had instinctively followed the path of Christian patriotism, bravely standing for what he believed to be the right, while still truly loving his enemies among whom the Christian redemption of the young was as much part of his mission as among his own people and their friends. Thus the present reunion was not so much an emotional reconciliation as an inevitable carrying on of a Christian internationalism and supranationalism emerging from the logic of his ideas and his work. To the communist *mystique* and *internationale* he simply opposed the Christian, which not only transcended national frontiers but in its basis of the liberty and responsibility of the sons of God included every man of goodwill, whether he had been accorded the gift of Christian faith or not. It was an inclusive answer to the exclusive sectarianism of those whom he sought to conquer.

Internationalism was in fact from now onwards to mark ever more clearly the personal life and activities of Canon Cardijn and of the movement. Though now well into his sixties, the veteran founder—a name to conjure with among the mounting numbers of his disciples and the far greater number of those who understood the wide significance of his contemporary apostolate—was ready to face the discomforts and fatigues, inevitably associated for older people even in modern conditions of travel, of constant displacement across the face of the world. Here too his shrewd common-sense realism and good sense helped him and his movement enormously.

As always, a clear perception of the nature of the job which he had to do dictated his manner of living. The visitor to his home in Brussels sees two large and well-kept cars parked in the inner court of the building. His first thought might be that the Y.C.W. is making an honest penny by renting a home to some industrial neighbour. Not a bit of it. The man who insisted from the start that nothing was more important in the formation of the Jocist than the faithful and regular payment of the subscription, symbol of his freedom, his responsibility, his earnestness, has also always insisted on the proper tool for the job. Just as the order of his day, with sufficient rest and sufficiently early bed—no matter how important the would-be visitor may be—is sacred to him so that his output of daily work may be the highest possible, so the means of transport for someone called upon to be ever on the move within his own country or abroad must observe the principle of the conservation of energy. A careful calculation of the means necessary to attain the end has marked the whole career of the tough-headed Fleming, Joseph Cardijn. This realism in him is wholly acceptable and reassuring, for it goes with gentleness and charm which spring from the way in which he is always wedded to that end of his: utter service to others in realising the vision of Christ the Worker in the factories and workshops where workers can live lives in conformity with their tremendous status as sons of God. In earlier days, holy men could afford practices of abnegation which threw them on God's providence. Today, in a technocratic age, it is more a case of God helping those who help themselves, and the aid of God has certainly not been wanting to the boy and man who dedicated himself to winning the workers for God—and for themselves.

Cardijn, son of an illiterate father and a simple working-class mother, his first schooling being that of the poor children of Hal, was now attaining international renown for the social and spiritual value of his work. Already, just before the war, he entered into correspondence with the famous Nobel Prize winner and surgeon, Alexis Carrel, whose book *Man the Unknown* created interest all over the world. Carrel himself had become aware of the movement and its success, and he wrote a letter to its Founder in which he said: 'I have only just come into contact with the Y.C.W. movement. I had heard it spoken of, but was completely ignorant of its spirit and import: it is a new conception of life. The success of your organisation is one of the greatest events of our times.' Cardijn replied, sending him literature about the work. Two years later, in the first year of the war, Carrel wrote to tell him how much more he had learnt of 'the magnificent Movement of which you are the Founder'. He went on: 'My admiration for this Movement created by you has not ceased to grow stronger every day since then. I am writing now to ask you to send me the articles you have doubtless published during the last two years.' This letter led to their meeting in Paris, and, shortly after, Carrel wrote again to say : 'Since I had the good fortune of meeting you, I have thought of you and your magnificent work very often. I am struck more every day by the extraordinary greatness of this enterprise. If Christian inspiration succeeds in penetrating economic and social forms, likely to live on, it will perhaps build up a firm and indefinitely perfectible civilisation.'

The importance of Cardijn's initiative, so much praised by the popes and many bishops yet often coolly received at lower ecclesiastical and lay levels, was now to earn him university doctorate after university doctorate, especially in the New World, and the young enthusiast they had once laughed at in Louvain would soon be similarly honoured by that great Catholic university. As a matter of course, the movement was becoming officially affiliated not only to Catholic international youth, industrial Catholic Action, and social service organisations, but permanently represented in UNESCO, ILO and other inter-governmental organisations, as well as in non-governmental world organisations for youth and social questions. Ex-Jocists were now finding themselves in leading political roles in their countries.

All this attested not only the intrinsic value of the movement but its steady growth and importance all over the world. Within a few years of the ending of war the Y.C.W. was not only well established in practically every free country in Europe and in the Americas, but was already beginning to make progress in such Asian countries as India, Ceylon, and Japan. Progress in all these countries, though varying from one to another, was steady, and the first feelers were being made for a work that would grow ever more important in the Founder's eyes, namely in African and colonial territories where a new proletariat was rapidly being born, shackled not only by subhuman industrial and social conditions but by problems of race and colour.

Enormous as was the problem still presented by working youth in the West, especially from the Christian and human angle, it paled compared with the awakening of a new proletariat and the opening out of a new world overseas where, despite the relative fewness of Christians, the problem of human dignity and rights came fully within the scope of the movement. Conditions for success would be much harder, because the growth of the movement was bound to be slower, as the transition from underdevelopment to fuller development threatened even worse disasters—religious, political and social—than the western Industrial Revolution had witnessed. Here, more than ever, the strength of the Y.C.W. lay in that flexibility which its Founder had insisted on from the start. The principles remained valid everywhere: the 'See, Judge, Act', the 'with them, by them and for them', the all-importance of formation of leaders and chaplains; the primacy of the spiritual, yet understood in such a way as never to allow any divorce between the spiritual ideal and the here-and-now temporal ideal for the workers—the two being complementary. But the ways of applying them to conditions constantly differing from one another must be indefinitely varying.

Cardijn's insistence on the right formation and the delegation of responsibilities ensured from the start an authentic and successful Y.C.W. wherever the movement was established, yet in these years of indefinite world expansion, with the numbers rising above the million figure, there could be no greater tonic for the Young Christian Workers in every part of the globe than the presence of the Founder

himself to teach, inspire, advise and just to be *there* for however short a space of time. Equally, the Y.C.W. tradition
of great congresses and rallies as soon as numbers and
general interest warranted them inevitably raised hopes that
the Founder might be present on the great occasion. Hence
the fantastic world journeys of the ageing priest which
have become more and more part of his life during these
latter years.

They began with the 1947 tour to Canada (for a Y.C.W.
congress at Montreal), the United States, Mexico, Costa-
Rica, Panama, Peru, Chile, the Argentine, Uruguay and
back home via the United States. Cardijn was accompanied
by the British International Secretary, Pat Keegan.

The movement had been established many years in
Canada, and to Cardijn the week there, travelling all the
time to see as much of the work as possible, was more like a
home-coming. For the Y.C.W., the United States (delegates
of whose young Y.C.W. had gone to Montreal) was more
a country of the future, but one in which Cardijn rested
very great hopes. Travelling from the east coast to the
west, he was able to realise how welcome to a great country
with new ideas the missionary conception of the Y.C.W.
was. Cardijn himself was equally optimistic, saying: 'When
the Americans have fully understood this method and have
learnt to adapt it to their mentality and needs, their spirit
of initiative and their practical sense of the reality of things
will cause them to make a very great success of it.' From
that time the Y.C.W. in the United States (where the
men's and women's sections are more closely linked than in
the Old World) has made steady progress, having solidly
established itself in between thirty and forty of the country's
cities, with hundreds of sections.

After a few days' stay in Mexico, Cardijn took part in a
chaplains' study week in Costa-Rica where the movement
was held in high government esteem and where Cardijn

was greatly touched when the young nineteen-year-old Indian president of the Nicaragua Y.C.W., having journeyed 500 miles, presented him with a fine Y.C.W. plaque in silver worked by himself.

In the subsequent three-weeks tour of South America Cardijn was able to observe progress and development which was often startling in view of the relatively recent foundation of the movement. It must be remembered that for many reasons Catholic formation and social education among the workers there was far less developed than in North America and in Europe. The Y.C.W., though pioneering in Europe a new conception of apostolate, was by no means unique in interesting itself in the social formation of young workers. By comparison, in Latin America the Y.C.W. was an all-round pioneer movement and its first emphasis had to be on the groundwork of Christian and social formation. In Chile, for example, Cardijn was able to observe the beginnings of basic Christian training by the Y.C.W. for young people. Such young people had often never spoken to a priest and their education had hardly begun. It was absolutely novel work, beginning from the elements of education and elementary training in social values to retreats, holiday camps, the Christian settlement of workers, families, couples. Once again, the Y.C.W. was illustrating that inherent flexibility and capacity for adaptation which made it so outstanding. The advice and encouragement of its Founder enabled it to look forward to steady progress in filling a great Christian need.

The Argentine had been the first Latin American country to develop the movement, and progress was already manifest. In Buenos-Aires, Cardijn, as the outstanding pioneer of Christian social youth-work, was given a triumphant reception at the National Youth Congress, where 50,000 young people were present. His services were requested on all sides, and in his short visit he had to give conference after conference—to the clergy, to industrialists, to lay leaders, to his own Jocists.

Across the water, in Montevideo, he greeted the first Y.C.W. foundations in Uruguay. Time did not permit a visit to Brazil on this tour, and he flew back to New York to do a further rapid tour through the United States, speaking in Chicago, Detroit, Pittsburg, Providence and Woonsocket, Rhode Island. The Y.C.W. of New York and Brooklyn, strengthened by Canadian delegates, gathered together for his final departure. But his great tour was not yet finished.

England was on his agenda, and in London, Manchester and Liverpool meetings and conferences were arranged to greet the Founder and be inspired and directed in the expansion of the work. In London a particularly fruitful contact was made between Cardijn and Cardinal Griffin. The Cardinal was deeply impressed by his dynamic personality and by the aims of the movement, especially to form Catholic working-class leaders. Cardijn was no less impressed by the mind and energy of the young Cardinal, for he would afterwards often cite Cardinal Griffin's approval and encouragement as an outstanding note in the movement's development. Cardijn as a young man had learnt much from Britain and he set high hopes, in his later years, on progress in so highly-industrialised and socially-advanced a country.

At length his 30,000-mile tour was over; and, in his own words, feeling 'squeezed like a lemon', he was back in his Brussels home.

Reviewing his experiences, he said:

I could never have believed that the Y.C.W. was so well-known, so much loved and so eagerly awaited in the States of the three Americas. Far greater than I would have expected was the greeting I received—greeting from the Hierarchy, the young workers, men and women, and the working-class leaders. It became evident to me that the problem of the worker and especially the problem of the young woman worker is a world-problem. It exists as much in the frozen poles as in the bush of the equator, in the sprawling cities as in the immense plantations, among whites as among the coloured. Certainly there are slight differences, but they are accidental. Essential and outstanding are the basic conditions: insecurity, lack of dignity and of respect for the human person and the family, misery face to face with excessive wealth, a psychological sense of inferiority and of being exploited. Face to face with this urgent, essential world-problem stands the Jocist solution—positive, practical and complete: working youth itself in action, by it, with it, for it, forming itself and organising itself for life, there where life is lived and where the masses are, guided by militants and leaders who are responsible and influential, united together and with the masses. I cannot repeat it too often: such is the only efficacious and salutary revolution. We have nothing to do with revolutions by violence, hatred, murder and destruction. We are the revolution by a new youth and a new working class, with new men, with the conception—the *mystique*—of a new life. There and there only will salvation be found. The fate of the young worker and of the whole world's working class is in our hands. How often I have trembled at the thought of this responsibility. If only all our militants, our leaders, our chaplains could share my conviction! Such is the greatest grace I ask of God after this great tour. And now more than ever back to work for the saving of youth and the working class of the world.[1]

These words express the exaltation and faith of the sixty-five-year-old leader after the great 'See; Judge; Act' of his journey. To set his sights so high may seem a little strange when across 30,000 miles of country the Y.C.W., however remarkable its progress, was only a small series of pin points. But Cardijn, as ever, was seizing the true size of the problem to be solved and realising that it could never be solved save

[1] *Cardijn*, p. 48.

by a Christianity deployed and in action across the face of the world, a Christianity wherein Church and people move together in harmony, understanding and shared responsibility according to a true and valid plan. For such stood the Young Christian Workers.

Cardijn's resolution, faith and optimism in the face of the problem of the post-war world were, after all, no greater in 1947 than they had been in Hal, in Malines, in Basse-Wavre, in Louvain and, above all, in Laeken when, in the face of disinterest, criticism and opposition, he solidly built against all odds the foundation of a movement whose progress had been so remarkable.

'They try to kill me, but they don't succeed,' he said after the tour, in reference to the work he had been called to do wherever he stopped during his journeying. Yet that tour was only typical of the travelling and the work he was to get through during the coming years when most men would be planning, after a hard life, a gentle retirement.

II

JUBILEE INTERNATIONAL
(1950)

ANNIVERSARIES and jubilees were succeeding one another ever more rapidly in the story of the Y.C.W., international and national, and each one served to rally members and fill them with fresh courage and enthusiasm. But inevitably outstanding was the movement's Silver Jubilee, the anniversary in 1950 of its twenty-five years of official existence.

When Canon Cardijn in January 1949 paid his unofficial *ad limina* visit to Rome to report on his journeys—he had since been to Africa, linked closely to Belgium through the Belgian Congo where the movement had made an early start—he was able to tell the Pope of the preparations for the Silver Jubilee. 'I told the Pope that we were beginning our lengthy preparations at Easter with our regional leaders, men and women, for the Jubilee Year. Of his own accord, the Pope said: "I wish, myself, to share in these preparations for your Jubilee Year." ' And true to his word, Pius XII sent Cardijn a personally signed letter. 'I never thought he would send me an autographed letter,' Cardijn said. 'I thought he would follow the usual procedure: good wishes through his Secretary of State, Mgr. Montini. But he himself, favouring us in quite an exceptional way, wanted to write and sign this letter which will be one of the finest, the best, the Y.C.W. has ever received from the Sovereign Pontiff.' [1]

In it the Pope said:

Who would have thought that when a quarter of a century ago you established on Belgian soil in the midst of innumerable difficulties and contradictions the first foundations of this building, it would grow in so few years to such vast size and so soon spread, not only in Belgium but in many nations of Europe and even as far as America and nearly throughout the world? The truth is that it came at its destined hour in the plans of Providence to help solve a problem not confined to any one region or province: the problem that nowadays faces the Christian conscience, of the fate of so many workers threatened in the most precious of their possessions, namely their faith in God, their supernatural life and the eternal salvation of their souls. The ideal which from the start moved you and which you understood how to spread through thousands of good and generous hearts was to give Christ and the Church back to them, starting with the young. The results stand before us as we look. They are those admirable cohorts of young leaders, men and women, of which the Church is so proud, for she sees in them the promise and guarantee of the re-Christianisation of the world of the workers.

And the Pope added:

The situation at the present moment at this decisive turning point in history demands that apostolate today more than ever. We shall never resolve these problems by any negative or merely defensive attitude towards the bad shepherds. This will only be done through the active presence within factories and workshops of pioneers who fully realise their dual vocation—Christian and worker—and who have made up their minds to accept the responsibilities lying on their shoulders, knowing neither truce nor rest, until the day when they have transformed the *milieu* where they live and work according to the demands of the Gospel. Only through this positive and constructive work will the Church be able to spread its life-giving action to the millions of souls for whom

she has so ardent and motherly a care. To such a sublime task
are called the young Christian-worker leaders formed by the
Y.C.W.

This personal Papal letter to Cardijn is one of the clearest
and most forthright expressions of the nature of the
Christian apostolate in the conditions of the present time.
Addressed to the Founder of the Y.C.W. and expressed in
terms of that pioneer movement, its message is nevertheless
applicable to Catholics and Christians all over the world.
The time has come, Pius XII says in effect, to lift that
defensive state of siege which the success of the Reformation
brought in its train, and to embark everywhere on Christian
missionary work, 'positive and constructive', which can
alone save a paganised world. It is a responsibility that falls
on each and every Christian.

By every action and the simplest of his actions [Cardijn said],
each young worker has, every day, a job to do—just as the
Pope himself has, as the bishops, as the priests, as the religious,
as the statesmen. They all have their job. This is a job which
lasts through the years of youth and throughout life, in the
family, in social relationships, in the period of being engaged,
in marriage, in work and leisure. And each young worker
must do that job *himself*, knowing its value and understanding
its importance. No one can do it for him, any more than anyone can get another person to do his washing and eating for
him. I underline this point strongly: no one can take the place
of the young worker, not even the good Lord, not even our
Saviour Jesus Christ, not even the Pope, the bishops, the
priests, the religious, no one.[1]

Cardijn, moved by the post-war state of the world and his
long journeys across the world, was obviously deeply conscious before and through the Jubilee of the full nature of
the Christian missionary apostolate. The conferences he
gave at this period have an 'all or nothing' character. He

[1] *Le Jeune Travailleur* (1949), p. 6.

seemed to be envisaging an unprecedented opportunity and unprecedented risks.

In 1948, in his conferences on The Hour of the Working Class, he explained to his leaders how industry was developing in South America and Africa. 'Neither the Church nor humanity itself can progress,' he told them, 'if we cannot persuade the working class to accept its responsibilities for the world's future, for the Church, for production. The working class is of age. Without it the Church can no longer accomplish its mission. The Church without the working class is not the Church of our Saviour Jesus Christ.'

Reporting to the Pope, he explained how today the Church had to have two different kinds of missionaries.

There are what the Pope calls the missionaries for the exterior, those who go to China, Japan, the Congo and other distant lands to convert pagans. Side by side with them, however, there are also the missions and the missionaries for the interior. And the Pope adds 'the missions of the interior are often tougher and more important than the missions of the exterior'. By missions for the interior the Pope means missions for all those sections of the population which are slipping more and more away from the Church, which are far from it and, like pagans, outside the Church: worker *milieux*, worker worlds into which the Church cannot penetrate and where it has no influence. For these we must organise today missions of the interior and missionaries of the interior. To succeed here there must be a missionary movement—not just on a diocesan or national scale, but on a world scale—for these millions of workers whom the Church does not reach, but which the Church must include if she is to fulfil her mission.

Conditioned by his own history and conscious always of his own special call, Cardijn always stressed the importance of his workers—and with good cause in view of their numbers and the trend of the times; but it is obvious that his words applied also to every other section of Christian people, to peasants and workers on the land, to soldiers and sailors, to students and intellectuals, to professionals, even to employers. It applied to the older as much as to the younger, though Cardijn always remained true to his maxim of 'catch them young'. Because of this, when we think of Cardijn and his Y.C.W., we have to think also of the large number of other up-to-date lay missionary and apostolic bodies which have been founded to apply in other sections of Catholic people the principles which Cardijn, at one time almost alone, pioneered. And since the formation, spiritual and temporal, of leaders is at the heart of his movement, we cannot but link his work with the great spiritual and educative innovations of our time within the Church.

In his 1949 conferences on The Young Worker Facing Life,[1] Cardijn hammered again and again at the most vital point and (in the modern Church) most novel point of his work: the individual responsibility (which is another word for individual missionary action) of each and every person.

Each young worker, man and woman [he said], has, as every human person has, a divine part to play, a part on which depends the fulfilment of the divine plan for the never-ceasing creation and redemption of the world. . . . But, in practice, do many Christians believe in this basic truth of their religion? . . . I must confess that during my recent journeys the thought has often come to me: 'It is not Christians I am meeting, but Pharisees.' They have no belief in the personal dignity of every young worker, of those boys and girls of the Indies, of Africa, of Japan.

And once again he taught the way.

It is not good enough to educate young people of the working classes in Catholic schools from six to fourteen and then to forget them in the factory, at work, away from school, away

---

[1] Quotations in this chapter, unless otherwise noted, are from this lecture.

from their parents. Even if they have been in the best of Catholic schools, even if they have been daily communicants, they are lost if they are abandoned after that. . . . Just as you cannot have priests without seminaries or religious without noviceships, so you can never have young Christian workers without forming them. Useless to hope for it; it is absolutely impossible.

Strong, daring and categorical words which too few have taken seriously.

Of the Y.C.W. itself at work he said—and what he said is, once again, universally applicable to all apostolic Christianity:

> The Y.C.W. is essentially, continually, everywhere and before all a recruitment. . . . What is the essential characteristic of every Jocist? It is the spirit of recruiting, the missionary spirit, the apostolic spirit, always drawn outwards towards others, never turned in on oneself. . . . Recruitment is for the Mystical Body of Christ that it may grow and become greater, gradually approaching the size of humanity itself so that both, humanity and the Mystical Body, become truly one.

And moved once again by his experiences across the world, he added: 'Never say, *a priori*, not the Chinese, the Japanese, the Africans, the Indians, but only the Europeans. In the Y.C.W. that is false.'

Explaining what he meant by formation, he contrasted it with the totalitarian dressage or breaking-in, telling them that he could go on for hours frightening them with descriptions of how men can be broken-in today. 'Faced with this dressage, we can only have one solution: it is not enough to teach or to pass on a doctrine. We must give a formation which is something quite other than just teaching. It is to learn how to act: to act through love, and freely; to know how to suffer and fight for this. There is no other cure and solution against the régime of dictatorship and dressage.'

And Cardijn, returning once again to his central spiritual teaching, demanded an 'apostolic spirituality'.

It is not your business to imitate priests and religious. You are lay-people, young workers, engaged couples—tomorrow, fathers, wives, mothers. . . . The worker's tool stands in his hand as the chalice and the paten in the hands of the priest. Just as the priest offers the Body and Blood of Christ on the paten and in the chalice, so the worker-apostle must learn to offer to Christ, in and with his tools, the sufferings of Christ, the tiredness and weariness of Christ with which he is united as part of the Mystical Body. . . . It is not a question in the factory of having a rosary or a missal in one's hands. In the factory the tools of the job are in one's hands. You have to work; but you have also to learn a spirituality in which one's work becomes one's prayer. Our work should be a continuous Mass in union with the priest at the altar. The hosts are the millions upon millions of workers in the workshops, the offices, the factories, and they are all placed on that paten by the side of the great Host which is Christ. . . . There is no religion to one side of life—no prayer to one side of life. Such prayer, such religion, would be false. Prayer and religion must transform life, make life divine, re-link the lives of men to the life of God.

Finally, at the beginning of the Jubilee Year, he called for 'a new apostolic move-forward' in response to the Pope's call.

True to his lifelong way of seeing and doing things, Cardijn, in grasping the immense scale of the post-war need, demanded a new effort on a similar scale. Nothing could ever deter him.

Cardijn's increasing sense of a whole world at stake, of the 'all or nothing' stakes of the day, of what he called 'the providential hour of the laity', was even more clearly expressed in the addresses he gave to the men and to the women Jocists at Easter 1950 on the eve of the Jubilee Congress.

> This Congress [he told them], if it is not to be just bluff, just a noise, a passing, morrow-less thing, must be something of which we can thoroughly understand the importance. To be able to understand that importance, we must also understand the basic truths we are spreading across the world—truths that are not superficial, but absolutely vital truths, the most important of all and for which we must be ready to die. We live at a decisive stage in the evangelisation of the world. It is a question of the Gospel of Christ adapted to the conditions of 1950, the Gospel which God calls upon us to proclaim and, as apostles and missionaries, to live. Equally must we be convinced that the truths we are going to proclaim are the key to all human happiness. No happiness, no freedom, no salvation for the world without them. . . . Essential truths and revolutionary truths, not just because they lead to reforms, but because they change basically the personalities of millions alive today.[1]

He contrasted the way in which the apostolic Catholic must be ready to live and die for these truths with the superficial detachment with which great world institutions like the United Nations pay lip-service to its principles.

Addressing the women in particular, he said, in the light of his travels:

> These truths are especially important for women. Today in the world there are 1,200 million women and girls. After travelling through a few countries one appreciates what these truths mean to women. For example, there are 350 million Moslems: think how women are treated in those countries. Go to India, China, Japan and most Asian and African countries and see. It is a case of the woman, the girl, far more than of the man—that she may have the chance of a happy life as woman and as young girl. . . . Whether it be a case of the poor Chinaman, of the Indian, of the 1,200 million women

[1] *La Personne, La Famille, L'Education*, p. 54.

and children, in the case of all and each of them this truth remains essential in every age and in every condition. As much in the worker, man and woman, as in a king or an empress—in the perverted and corrupt man as well as in the woman for whom all seems lost, the prostitute, the woman of bad life—in all of them there exists a dignity which the whole world must respect, even if it has to take measures against them. In my view, to realise this is the most important conviction at the present time and in the world that is evolving through the coming years and during the next half-century. This truth can be expressed in a few words: every worker, man and woman, as with every human being, is a *person*—a person like the three Divine Persons, yes, a *person*.

And after an explanation in biological, moral and theological terms of what a person is, Cardijn concluded:

Today we have reached in world history what may be called 'the hour of the person'. It is an hour when, on the one side, there are great possibilities and, on the other, the greatest possible dangers. Hence it is a providential and revolutionary hour. That is why our Congress has come at the providential moment: the hour of the human person without distinction of race or continent, the same human person in all conditions without exception. All must be saved and all can be saved. . . . Today, thanks to air-travel, one can go anywhere. Radio, cinema, technology link all together. Today all the persons of the world can be reached and all can be told that they possess the dignity of man.

Some may feel that there is a certain simplicity, a certain naïvety, in Cardijn's message with its hammering of simple basic truths and its optimistic expectations. But where others, more intellectual perhaps, dwelt on the complexities and distinctions of philosophy and theology, the largely self-taught Fleming moved hundreds of thousands by hammering again and again on fundamentals, expressed with the utmost clarity and applied practically through the force of

his personality and the simple basic principles of his movement. To grasp the roots and imaginatively appreciate the
contemporary possibilities of planting and spreading those
roots in a new world was his special strength. How necessary his approach was, and remains, becomes clear when we
realise that the vast majority of Christians, let alone others,
in the world still by-pass these fundamentals and fail to see
the opportunities, content to live largely self-regarding
spiritual lives by mere force of habit.

Still bold, even in 1950, was Cardijn's insistence on the
role of the laity in the Church, as he concluded these
conferences in preparation for the Jubilee Congress. Seeing
in a new apostolic laity the real answer to 'the great heresy
of laicism', he explained how the lay world was more and
more drifting away from any religious influence.

A whole lay world of science, of technology, of economics, of
finance and commerce, of literature, of art, of civic life, of
politics is becoming a world closed to the Church's influence.
Religion may be thought a good thing in church, in its worship and sacraments; but religion no longer enters into life
itself, into the living, temporal, scientific, technical world, and
the Church no longer exerts its influence on the world of work
or, above all, on the world of the workers, though the number
of these is increasing prodigiously in all the continents.
Against this 'laicism', the Pope, the bishops, the priests and
religious cannot immediately react. They cannot directly
influence that lay world simply because they themselves are
not lay people. They can and must give to the world the
Person of Christ, his doctrine and his grace, but they cannot
themselves spread these wherever the people live. It is the
laity that must help the Pope, the bishops and the priests to
save the lay world, to penetrate into and rechristianise the
world of work. . . . We have reached the providentially
destined hour of the laity in the Church, the hour of the
apostolate of the lay people in the Church. We must make all
the faithful—bachelors, married, workers, employers, scien-

tists, doctors—understand afresh that they have an apostolate
to carry out, that they must be missionaries. . . . The hour
of the worker is also the hour of worker-apostolate—not just
a haphazard, scattered apostolate, but an organised apostolate. . . . The rechristianisation of the world must be tackled
so that men may again know the message of Christ, feel themselves to be sons of God and co-workers with God, and realise
that they are called to be heirs of God. Such is the meaning
of this Congress.[1]

And Cardijn explained the purpose and time-table of the
Jubilee manifestations. First the opening with the con-
secration of all to the Blessed Virgin. Why the Blessed
Virgin? Because Mary was a poor young girl of the people,
a young worker, engaged to a worker, the wife of a worker,
the mother of a worker family who throughout her life
remained of the workers in her humble home of the worker-
world of her day. Yet 'without the Blessed Virgin, no
Christ, no apostle, no Pope, no bishop, no priest, no
religious'. In the hour of laity 'the Blessed Virgin, together
with her divine Son, will play an ever-greater *avant-garde*
role in order to demonstrate the extraordinary nature of the
vocation which God has reserved to man and to woman in
the execution of his divine plan'. Here Cardijn was echoing
the practical down-to-earth spirituality with which he had
countered Marxism in the past. To understand Catholic
devotion to our Lady we do not need to look up to the
Queen of Heaven, but down to a Jewish worker-girl whose
work made possible the Incarnation and the Church.

Then the solemn Mass sung by a hundred thousand young
workers and relayed into hundreds of thousands of homes
by radio—the Mass that would stand as witness to the one
Saviour of the workers: Christ the Worker who alone can
save the workers today and resolve all the problems of the
hour.

[1] *La Personne, La Famille, L'Education*, pp. 46–8.

In the afternoon, in the great Olympic Stadium of Brussels, Jocists from forty-two countries, represented by 500 delegates from among the 100,000 filling the stadium, would themselves deliver to the world the Y.C.W. message: the problem of the workers of the world who, if they cannot be saved, must be condemned to remain the damned of the earth, the prisoners of hunger, threatened with slavery all the more because of progress, technology and science. No cardinal would deliver that message, but the workers themselves, of every race and colour, of every land and continent.

Intimately bound up with the Congress manifestation must be the International Conference, lasting a week and attended by delegates from all over the world. The Conference would have no meaning without the public witness and solemn engagement of the Congress manifestation. The Congress could never do its work unless its spirit were translated into practical action by the International Conference. 'We have no use for a merely national spirit; we want a catholic spirit, a universal spirit. It is the entire world which we must save and conquer.'

The studies of the 1950 International Conference which took place in September have been reported in the valuable Y.C.W. book, *Une Etape de L'Internationale Jociste*, and even a hurried glance at those 300 pages demonstrates both the scope and the 'down to earth' character of the movement which Cardijn founded. Describing the pre-Jubilee conferences given by the Founder, we may have given the impression that Jocism was becoming concentrated on its spiritual approach. Cardijn is the Chaplain-General and he takes his own place in the movement with the other vitally necessary chaplains whose role it is to inspire, train and provide the basic spiritual motive without which Jocism would have no meaning. But the report of the Jubilee Conference makes crystal-clear what is still the determining and almost unique mark of the Cardijn work, namely the serious and detailed grappling with the concrete social problems of the workers today as realistically and uncompromisingly as any political or socialist movement. Cardijn has never flinched from this practical and temporal aim as necessarily inspired by a proper appreciation of the meaning of Christianity in the world today. He started out as still hardly more than a boy to save the working class; he has never allowed his movement to be sidetracked into the easy but purposeless road of remaining, as a Catholic movement, at the plane of devotional and spiritual self-polishing.

On the basis of 'See and Judge', the Conference with its globe-scattered delegates reported on the actual conditions of workers all over the world, on their education, their housing conditions, their techniques, their health, the degree of responsibility and autonomy which they possessed, as well as their religious and moral lives. 'Judging', they were able to consider the necessary shaping and formation of their movement in relation to the precise conditions which obtained in all the countries represented.

Even more impressive, perhaps, is the sense which the Conference report conveys of the international character which the movement had acquired in only twenty-five years—and in this it was absolutely unique in the world as an international answer to international communism. Indeed, it was far more truly international than communism, since the latter was as much a political agency of an imperialist and totalitarian Great Power as a genuine workers' movement. The Y.C.W. had no national attachment, its inspiration being solely the universal Church. In the pages of the report can be found what are surely unique reports in detail of every aspect of the workers' lives in fifty countries, including small and obscure countries of South America, Africa and Asia.

Perhaps the heart of the Y.C.W. social ideal is given

in the following paragraphs, based on a genuine world survey:

For a long time the working class has had to be satisfied with demanding material, social and political advances: social security, the eight-hour day, universal suffrage and the rest.

Today the time has come when it can and must share in the direction of production and the administration of its own interests. We can no longer imagine a world still moving towards progress and unity without the working class, now spread everywhere and organised, having its true share of responsibility.

The working class cannot escape from these responsibilities without handing over the world of today, as well as the unknown possibilities of the future, to anarchy and sterility.

Above all, it cannot accept or claim these responsibilities without the most thoughtful facing up to them. The working class must make a tremendous effort to form worker-leaders who will prove competent and influential, capable of assuming and successfully realising the grand and heavy tasks that will fall on their shoulders. To insist upon such leadership in so topsy-turvy a world and at so grave an hour would be a crime against the working class itself unless sufficient preparations were made to ensure a conscientious and competent use of power and the will to seek the common good in a task of such dimensions. Indeed that would be a form of deliberate suicide and a direct call for dictatorship regardless of its source.[1]

[1] *Une Etape de L'Internationale Jociste*, p. 107.

12

THE SECRET OF CARDIJN
(1950–)

THE Jubilee Congress and International Conference which took place two months before Cardijn entered his seventieth year may fitly be taken to be the crown of his life's work. By the Pope he was honoured with the title of Monsignor. His own country made him a Commander of the Order of Leopold, while France, where his movement had come to to be of such importance in the work of spiritually undermining the immense hard core of secularism in the working class and in promoting similar apostolic movements of an interior and lay missionary character, gave him the Legion of Honour.

The little, poor boy from Hal who wanted to save his worker friends from the corruption of workshop and factory life had grown into one of the half-dozen most significant Catholic leaders in the world.

The young clerical student of Malines and schoolmaster of Basse-Wavre, who had scandalised his fellow-clergy in pursuing political and social causes that seemed alien to his high spiritual vocation, had lived to speak on platforms and rallies in all parts of the world in defence of the Christian social rights of the workers of all races and conditions.

The new curate of Laeken, expected to fall into the customary parochial round of flattering the bourgeois devout and less devout and chiding the tough and slack, had raised a new class, gathering the humble apprentices and young workers, expected to maintain their lowly

station, into a proud and effective organisation which gave
them an unprecedented sense of self-respect, Christian
dignity and capacity. In the face of misunderstanding and
criticism from high and low, the self-constituted apostle of
the young and of the workers had journeyed to an unknown
Rome to be embraced by the Pope, to be told that he alone
was doing what in present times all others should be doing,
saving the masses when the best insisted on concentrating
only on the apparently best. His strange movement,
scarcely fitting into any accepted pattern, half-spiritual,
half-temporal, ecclesiastical yet political, clerical but un-
precedentedly and uncompromisingly lay, was approved
and destined to be the model of the contemporary apostolic
method called 'specialised Catholic Action'.

Its potentiality in the spiritual order was to prepare the
way for the rapid increase in the Church of the adaptation
of the methods and use of public worship to the needs of the
new worker-people, unlettered in the old sense, ill-
instructed in the minutiae of catechism and ritual, separate
from clerical and school masters. To these new masses,
seeking vainly in the old classical order of Church life the
religious expression of their idealism, the Church was bringing what Cardijn had taught from the beginning: a living
relationship between liturgical and sacramental life and the
daily sacrifice of their hands and muscles on the altar of
industrial work. The Mass is ended: go and make your day
a continual Mass in union with the Mass offered by the
Pope, the bishops, the priests, the Mass whose effects are
confirmed in all your lives. Without your work there could
be no Mass, no bread, no wine, no paten, no altar.

Its potentiality in the spiritual and temporal organic
unity, which the Cardijn movement taught, was to prepare
the way for the new apostolate: the apostolate of a formed,
proud and responsible laity witnessing to Christ and the
dignity of the human person in the concrete circumstances

of workshop and factory, not by preaching, but by example and Christian leadership in actually changing bad conditions of social and industrial life into conditions consonant with the dignity and responsibility of sons of God.

Mgr. Cardijn in his seventieth year and the twenty-fifth of the official existence of the Y.C.W. movement could look around him and be amazed at the worker-army he had created, some two million strong and established in some seventy countries. God, he felt, had singularly, almost miraculously, blessed the work which he had inspired and which had been carried into such fruitfulness by his leader-disciples, following in the footsteps of the first three musketeers, Tonnet, Garcet, Meert. Cardijn himself was too modest to dwell on the other aspects of his work which so forcefully strike the outsider, the effect of the Y.C.W. initiative on the whole life of the Church today in its liturgical developments, bringing Church and people into closer and more active union, and the new lay missionary spirit in fresh movements and organisations which owe so much, often without realising it, to the ideas which the curate of Laeken was working out for himself near the beginning of the present century.

We do not propose to carry the details of the Cardijn story right up to the present moment. Nor is it necessary. Cardijn himself has not allowed age to diminish his activities, even though these are planned in the realistic Cardijn way to enable him to conserve his strength as well as may be. Only such planning could have allowed him to continue his world tours. In the one, for example, which immediately followed the Jubilee Congress, he thoroughly studied both the religious and the social situation in the countries of South America, finding them both deeply unsatisfactory, yet understanding the immense Christian promise which they offered. Hard realism was always combined with the highest idealism in his life's work.

The pictures which haunt us [he wrote home from Chile] are in keeping with the monstrous size of these countries. Shadows cover miseries, disorders and dangers which seem insurmountable; but lights reveal riches, possibilities, promises that could save the world. Among the shadows we find the personalist, demagogic, unstable régimes, having nothing of democracy but the name. . . . There is the population, superficial, uncultured, incapable of sustained effort, drawn to an over-populated capital. . . . There is the poverty of the clergy unable to answer the needs of the people, heaped up in the urban parishes or dispersed in rural ones as large as Belgium.

Among the lights he included

the inexhaustible wealth of the country capable of welcoming and feeding hundreds of millions more inhabitants; the people themselves who, though over-excitable and sometimes driven by passion, are good, generous and welcoming. Above all, despite the poverty of the clergy and religious ignorance, there is an attachment, a devotion, a deep confidence in our Lady, the Mother of God, whose protection is invoked by the masses with an unshakeable piety.

The 'See; Judge; Act' remains the Cardijn formula for himself, but now on a world scale. It thus contributes to the movement something which no one else could give—the veteran Founder himself personally observing even in the smallest details conditions of the Church and of social and economic life in every part of the globe, and on the basis of this continuous observation directing and adapting the international movement to all the vastly different needs. Where in America or Britain a grave Y.C.W. problem might be the Christian use of the leisure which shorter working hours and better financial conditions make possible, in the Philippines, which Cardijn visited in January 1954, it was a question of *chic* Y.C.W. girls in salmon frocks coping with workers who worked seven days a week from 7 a.m. to 6.30 p.m. and lived in houses like chicken coops, sleeping on shelves of wood. During this journey to Japan, via India and the Philippines, Cardijn, with the International President, Pat Keegan, was able to see Nehru, to whom he explained the movement, its story and its achievements. Everywhere in India, the Y.C.W. visitors saw evidence of the strength of communist progaganda, based, not so much on any ideology, but on the failure to cope with bad living and working conditions, Christianity itself, together even with the Indian Y.C.W., having too often a Western and Anglo-Indian background to wield a full social force on the working people. Fear of forming and trusting the workers in the Y.C.W. spirit, they thought, accounted for weakness in the Church's influence. Consolation was to be had on the round trip in Tokyo where, despite language difficulties of priests trained for the Chinese missions, a meeting with 180 Y.C.W. leaders, with the archbishop in the chair, gave hope of great future developments in Japan.

Cardijn, ever an observer and experimentalist, thoroughly enjoys even in his seventies these world tours, his eyes and young heart ever attentive to what excites the ordinary tourist as well as to the graver matters of the apostolate. So long as the world of his apostolate moves forward, so will he. His movement is such that every fresh development in social questions inevitably engages the attention of an organisation whose simple basic principles commit it to action and apostolate. Thus today when the racial question stands out as a problem of increasing gravity, demanding a solution if the underdeveloped parts of the world are not to fall victims to materialistic and communist fallacies, Cardijn, asked for his views about the problem by the International Institute of Differing Civilisations, can point to the declaration made by the Y.C.W. at the Jubilee International Congress:

'We once again proclaim that every young worker, man

and woman, of every country, every race, every religion, with no exception whatsoever, possesses a human and inviolable dignity, possesses a personal and communitarian mission and needs to be formed so that it can give itself over to that mission and responsibility.'

It was typical that Cardijn did not have to give a new answer to a new problem; he could, as always, give an old answer of his own and of his movement, for all sane international and social principles were envisaged in its Christian-social ideology. And this particular declaration, he pointed out, was subscribed to, not by academic professors, but by young Christian workers who, when they mounted the Jubilee Conference platform, received the most enthusiastic applause: the delegate of Gabon; the young founder of the movement in Japan; the young worker of Mozambique with the shame of the abuses of the marriage dowry upon him.

Today [Cardijn went on], the Y.C.W. has penetrated into more than seventy countries of all continents, gathering together millions of young workers of both sexes with an ideal of mutual help, of love for one another, of solidarity, of mutual respect, all based on their divine origin and destiny, all children of the same Father, brothers together in the one human community, having no racial prejudice, but intent, with irresistible passion and patience, to raise up even the poorest, the humblest, the most abandoned.

And he could point out many practical examples of how the movement tackled in the concrete the racial problems of the world. Pine House in New York where over 3,000 women workers of all races and types enjoyed life together—in the case of many of the coloured, for the first time—in a community without social and racial distinctions; in the Congo, where Belgian and native leaders worked together in the native city of Leopoldville—three white Belgians alone in a coloured community of 300,000; in a Senegal quarry, where a single French Jocist had been working for two years with the natives, adapting himself to their way of life and amazing them by refusing to allow himself any difference at all between his own way of life and theirs.

Sixty different Y.C.W. publications, produced all over the world, continuously report the practical work of living together without any trace of racial discrimination, egoism, or prejudice, while the movement in European and North American countries maintains relations of friendship and practical assistance with their brothers and sisters all over the world.

In this example of the Y.C.W. record, it is not a question of the Y.C.W. doing things that are not done by many other people and societies in the world. But what must impress the observer of the movement and student of the work of its Founder is the virtually automatic way in which the Y.C.W. can show itself to have the practical and lived answer to social and applied spiritual problems of every kind. It is all in the *Manuel*; it was all thought out by Cardijn in the prison of Saint-Gilles during the First World War, not necessarily by name, but in terms of applied Christian principle of life in the twentieth century so complete and so logical that his followers automatically react in the truly Christian way to each fresh problem as it arises, and usually well before it has become news.

This record involves nothing miraculous, nor does it suggest exceptional intellectual powers either in the Founder or among his followers. We have seen that Mgr. Cardijn was by no means an exceptionally gifted person in the academic intellectual sense, while his education was by no means first-class. Nor do his followers, even those in high positions, necessarily strike the outsider as academically intelligent trained minds. They may be; they may not be.

The secret is far more simply explained. What Cardijn

did and what Cardijn has throughout his life taught his disciples to do is *to use and apply* in the most practical and commonsense fashion the tradition and wisdom enshrined in the revelation and experience of the Catholic Church itself.

As a boy and a young man, he was educated and formed in a Church the vast majority of whose members, clerical and lay, did not think of applying the person of Christ, the teaching of the Gospels and the academically worked out spiritual and moral doctrine of the Catholic Church to the people of the world in their individual and social lives, even to the Catholic people of the world. Despite the efforts of popes, bishops and pioneers, the example of Christ was mainly conceived as applying to what we can best describe as Sunday and personal religion. And in so far as the week-day living conditions of people were concerned, most Christians of influence not only accepted, but defended, an order of society which derived not from Christian inspiration, but from traditions and political, social and economic theories that were wholly secularist. God (except on Sundays and in personal morals) had been ousted from social relations in the West, and most Catholics, fearing (and not without due cause) the disorders likely to attend secularist revolt against a bad social order, thought it wisest to defend the devil you knew against the worse devil that might arise.

Cardijn had greater courage and greater faith than most and he was providentially gifted with exceptional powers of imagination, organisation and publicity. He was determined, in the vastly important field he understood best through his upbringing and associations, to form a Christian movement whose job it would be to bring Christ truly, realistically, almost scientifically, to the living people, to apply the truth, the idealism and wisdom of *total* Christianity to the real workaday world. It was a formula that could not in itself fail, given the necessary authentic spiritual inspiration and worldly experience of its Founder—could not fail, that is, unless his initiative was formally forbidden. And Pope Pius XI saw to it that it should not be forbidden.

There, it would seem, is the simple secret of Mgr. Cardijn and the Y.C.W., officially founded thirty-two years ago but prepared many years before. The simple secret having thus been revealed, it was equally inevitable that it should come to be increasingly applied and developed within the whole pastoral and apostolic work of the Church during the present century.

Herein really lies the answer to criticisms and disappointments about the Y.C.W. movement which are not rarely to be heard even today.

Mgr. Cardijn holds it to be providential that the Y.C.W. should have spread in thirty years all over the world, with numbers in the neighbourhood of two million, and we have seen that he founded the movement with the intention of conquering the world. Such progress is indeed extraordinary when we remember that the movement was the pioneer type of apostolate of like by like, of Catholic Action 'with them, by them and for them'. But to it we have, in fairness, to add all that has been achieved in the contemporary apostolate within the Church by other movements which have largely been inspired by the Y.C.W. We have, too, to note that the popular spiritual and liturgical movements of the modern Church which have been gradually enabling the laity to understand and participate actively in communal and parish worship have gone hand in hand with the apostolic and interior missionary techniques that have owed much to Mgr. Cardijn's initiative in establishing a productive marriage between the spiritual and the temporal.

All this having been said, we have also to realise that the beginnings of this contemporary Christian revolution were at first viewed with great alarm by many excellent

Catholics, priests and laity. Alarm and prejudice have by
no means died out since then. Yet this alarm and prejudice
must, in the nature of things, hold back the progress of the
movement, for it is not a mass movement to which members
merely belong or subscribe. It is a movement which
absolutely depends, as Cardijn has so often insisted, on
quality: quality of leaders and quality of chaplains. The
formation of leaders of the required stamp is a long and
difficult business and the recruitment of chaplains with a
deep understanding of the modern apostolate and their
vital role in it cannot progress quickly so long as the majority of the clergy are prejudiced or even uninterested and un-
comprehending. The Y.C.W. and comparable missionary
movements within the Church of today cannot progress
quicker than the supply of understanding and enthusiastic
chaplains, as well as of high-class leaders, allows. Not
brains, but the apostolic enthusiasm and imaginative understanding of the increasing importance of this missionary
apostolate, as so often and so eloquently preached by Mgr.
Cardijn himself throughout his life, are the ingredients
needed if the ambitions of Cardijn are to be realised. One
can only imagine the revolutionary results of the movement
if the Christian clergy and laity of the world could appreciate and share the imaginative apostolic zeal, the realism
and the understanding of human forces and needs in the
world today which move Cardijn and his followers.

In these pages we have time and again underlined what
seems to us the deepest contribution made by Mgr.
Cardijn, namely the fruitful marriage between the spiritual
and the social or temporal—a marriage which makes the
role of the priest in the modern apostolate all-important,
yet in such a way as also to make the role of the lay
organisation and leaders all-important and all-responsible
too. The priest forms modern apostles; the modern apostles,
properly formed, in Mgr. Cardijn's words, 'conquer'.

Mgr. Cardijn, as usual, expressed it best in an address to the clergy and chaplains during the 1935 Jubilee Congress of the Y.C.W.:

Today's laity, if not a new laity so far as its mind and being are concerned, is nevertheless a new laity in regard to its formation, its organisation, its utilisation. When Pius XI made this truth the master-principle of his pontificate, he revolutionised the Church. If only the clergy would understand how far this apostolic transformation of the whole Church carries—the Church which is the Mystical Body of Christ, all of whose members share in the conquering life of their Leader. This *unam, sanctam, catholicam and apostolicam* Church must be, being ceaselessly rebuilt by a priesthood of Catholic Action, under the authority of the bishops and the Pope. Such a clergy must ceaselessly help it to expand. This militant and conquering Church, under the inspiration of a Catholic Action clergy and with a laity more and more conscious of its apostolic calling, will possess a true *mystique* of conquest and a true dynamism of conquest against that paganism and barbarism which threaten more than ever before Christian civilisation. Let us pray that our priests in a living and sanctifying union may work together for the formation of that Catholic Action clergy which the Pope wants, which the Church calls for, which our times await.[1]

The problems of the Young Christian Workers' movement today remain considerable—as must be the case with any great dynamic *action* movement whose habit it is always to leap ahead of itself. We have just referred to the difficulty of obtaining a sufficient number of truly understanding chaplains. But this problem really springs from the deeper one of the inevitable slowness of the Church's general organisation to adapt itself to such rapidly changing conditions in the world of today. For example, Catholic formation generally, whether clerical or in schools, remains

[1] *Semaine d'Etudes Internationale*, pp. 285–6.

theoretical rather than active, practical, and based on the handing over of responsibility. It remains a formation for personal, private Christian lives rather than for making an apostolic social body. Only slowly does a contemporary *Incarnational* sense of Christianity spread, whether within the four walls of the church or outside them. To see work as prayer, since work is the basis of all human life rendered potentially supernatural because Christ became Man, is still unusual and viewed theoretically rather than practically. The Mystical Body is much talked of, but its actual implications are rarely appreciated. Christians still prefer to be *anti* this or that danger and error, whether communism or socialism or progressivism or non-Catholic religions and religious efforts, than to share Cardijn's way of working to eliminate the causes from which wrong or one-sided views and ideologies must come. Yet, of course, it is the fate of pioneers and pioneer movements to create their own difficulties through being in advance of their times. Cardijn, as we have more than once said, is content to be surprised by the amount that has been accomplished, within a few years as the history of the Church goes. No one has had a better training in possessing his soul in patience and looking to God for fruits consonant with the worth of any work.

Within the movement itself there are technical problems to be solved as time goes on. We mentioned earlier the problem of ensuring that the ground gained by the Y.C.W. in Catholic youth and the early years of life is not lost, at least in part, when the 'Christian Workers' are no longer 'Young'. Another is the strengthening of the international character of the movement which in this its first phase has necessarily been closely tied to Belgium. But of these and other 'loose ends' it can at least be said that they are very much in Cardijn's mind and in the minds of leaders of the movement. Not all can be done in the course of a single generation, and to imagine that it could be done would be a sign that the force of the original inspiration and *mystique* was weakening. It is not so.

But it is not with the as yet unresolved problems of to-morrow in this organic movement that we must bring these pages to an end. Happily, the whole world has been afforded the most striking of all public witnesses to the success of the Cardijn story in the World Rally of the Y.C.W. which took place in Rome in August of last year (1957).

After many months of intense preparation and the arrangement of mutual help through the whole organisation to defray the heavy expenses of travel from across the world, 32,000 Young Christian Workers, men and women, from over eighty countries demonstrated the Christian Worker unity which transcended national, racial and even ideological divisions. In the Eternal City, the savage rhythm of Senegalese dancers, the tattooed faces of girls from Ghana, Chinese from Hong Kong, bronzed faces from the disturbed Middle East, mingled with delegates from all countries of the Atlantic and Mediterranean seaboards. They were together to pay homage to the Vicar of Christ and to present to him detailed reports, based upon personal surveys of the conditions, spiritual and temporal, of the workers from the four corners of the globe.

In the Caracalla Baths, cultures were represented in the folklore of dance and song. At the Colosseum, the tradition of the Christian Church since the days of the early martyrs was re-enacted in the symbolic sacrifice of the Way of the Cross, and the common faith was witnessed to with 32,000 voices in the Creed. In St. Peter's, with a third of the numbers overflowing into the Piazza, in the presence of six cardinals and fifty bishops, Mass was celebrated at the papal altar—the Mass which, in Cardijn's words, 'unites you round the tomb of St. Peter and is the real purpose of your journey to Rome'. Later that same day, within the Piazza, the Young Workers with over 100,000 people gathering round them waited for the Pope as the history, social significance and progress of the movement was choreographically represented. The turning of the historic spot into an immense stage was unprecedented.

In his speech, Pope Pius XII called the Christian youth leaders 'a hope for the social future and the Christian regeneration of the working world'.

> You will show yourselves [the Pope continued] to be true sons of the Church in bringing to others as 'Jocist missionaries', exercising fully your responsibilities as Young Christian Workers, the salvation which has been announced to you. . . . The Y.C.W. possesses a method of proved worth, having demonstrated its power of adaptation to the most varied conditions. Its direct contacts with working realities enable it to outline in every case a complete plan of action, which corresponds to the needs of the situation, and to give its members and through them to all young workers, the most efficacious kind of aid. We wish then that the public authorities would give ever wider recognition to its services, and assure it, particularly in those regions where the urgency of some intervention with regard to education is especially felt, the material means necessary for this most important task. . . . Now as in the past we count on you and we expect great things of you.

The World Rally, thirty-two years after the official foundation of the movement and forty-five after Mgr. Cardijn himself began actively to fulfil his promise to his dying father to kill himself 'to save the working class of the world', would, Monsignor Cardijn hopes and believes, mark the end of his active life, enabling him to retire to prayer and contemplation. It is high time, he says, for retreat and recollection. From such intimate contact with God in his room high above Brussels and in the little ground-floor chapel that has witnessed so much of the Cardijn story, he will, he feels, best obtain the divine graces and blessings for all he holds dearest.

But those who know him best can only smile. Did he not say a few years ago: 'I started by thirteen years of failure. And now I have been trying for forty-one years. I still go on. We must be convinced that it is absolutely necessary and that we shall be doing it to the day of our death—for it *is* absolutely necessary.'

We may leave him, then, after taking a last look at him, standing erect in his black soutane, his close-cropped white hair crowning a smiling face, still full of the spirit of youth, against the background of serried rows of books and the spotless tidiness of his study in the Rue des Palais. To his followers he is 'The Founder' and, like all creative people, he holds a tight rein. As jealously as he guards what he has created—sometimes perhaps to the momentary vexation of younger folk—so does he guard those principles of trust in others, of delegated responsibility, of personal intimacy and love for all his collaborators, those highly placed in the movement and the lowliest, for his love today, as from the beginning, is rooted in love of Christ our Lord, mystically present in the Church and brother to every man and woman, however much the powers of this world may use and abuse them.

Among the last of his printed words before the August 1957 World Rally in Rome were the following—words which will surely be echoed by all who may have come to know Joseph Cardijn and the Young Christian Workers a little better.

May the working class of the world soon chant the Magnificat of its own faith in the immense mission confided to it by the Creator and Redeemer—that mission which has been restored to it thanks to the worker-apostolate which Christ has raised up in his Church. At this all-decisive hour we carry and spread that mission. May we respond to the Church's trust. May we keep faith with the whole working class of the world that waits.[1]

[1] *Les Travailleurs et Les Perspectives Mondiales de l'Apostolat*, p. 14.